Mary M. Bauer

D0106682

ADVENTURE PUBLICATIONS, INC.
CAMBRIDGE, MINNESOTA

DEDICATION

Hiking Minnesota With Kids was an incredible pleasure to hike and write, thanks in big part to my enthusiastic trail buds, Kenny, Shelly, Shirley, Ruth, Susie, Julie, Bev and Nancy who walked with me every step of the way. You guys rock! Thanks also to the Adventure Publications crew who didn't hike, but rather ran with me on this cool journey—I feel phenomenally blessed to work with such a team. And finally, thanks to all who purchase this book. I hope you and the kids enjoy these adventures as much as we did bringing them to you.

Book and cover design by Jonathan Norberg

Great Blue Heron photo copyright by Stan Tekiela, all other photos copyright by Mary M. Bauer

Copyright 2006 by Mary M. Bauer
Published by:
Adventure Publications, Inc.
820 Cleveland St. S
Cambridge, MN 55008
1-800-678-7006
www.adventurepublications.net
Printed in the United States of America
ISBN-10: 1-59193-135-5
ISBN-13: 978-1-59193-135-5

TABLE OF CONTENTS

INTRODUCTION

Do you know what's great? It's great to think there are kids who know what the cool mist from a waterfall feels like on their face. It's great to realize there are kids who know the taste of a tart wild strawberry, or the intoxicating fragrance of a forest after a crisp October frost, or the startled bark of a great blue heron. It's great to imagine there are kids who know what it's like to discover fresh deer tracks in the black soil, or how to identify an oak tree from a maple tree, or know why it's important to be good stewards of the land.

We've begun to realize how incredibly important interacting with the natural world is for all people, especially kids. Medical experts and researchers at Johns Hopkins University School of Medicine, the National Institutes of Health, and the U.S. Centers for Disease Control reveal that an alarming—and rapidly growing—number of our kids are overweight, depressed, anxious and overstressed because they sit in front of some type of screen, be it video games, computer or television, for four to six hours (on average) every single day. In this artificial environment, kids' minds and bodies atrophy from lack of exercise and the necessary stimuli provided by nature. It's a condition experts call Nature Deficit Disorder.

The good news is that it's easy to keep your kids from becoming a statistic. As an adult, you can help kids take charge of their lives and their health. Getting them onto the exciting and interesting hiking trails of Minnesota is the fun way to keep them healthy!

Minnesota has tons of great hiking places; however, the trips featured in this book are specially geared toward kids. They are:

- based on length (most are less than two miles long)
- relatively easy
- interesting and varied
- close to other attractions suitable for kids, with special emphasis on outdoor activities

Each trail description also notes whether the trail is baby stroller-friendly, the location of the nearest restroom and drinking water, motel and camping suggestions, dining opportunities with impromptu picnics in mind, phone numbers and/or websites for the area chamber of commerce, equipment rentals and much more.

As a mother who hikes with her kids (now adults), I also included lots of helpful information not found in other books, such as:

- what to do if/when your child comes into contact with poison ivy
- preventing and detecting dehydration
- first aid tips and resources for handling emergencies
- expert-recommended use of insect repellent and sunscreen
- and lots more

"Wonderful!" you say. "This is just the information I need to get my kids out on a hike." But hold on—there's more. The really cool thing about *Hiking Minnesota with Kids* is the scavenger hunts! Besides the obvious enjoyment of finding the item on your list, many of the items were chosen to encourage real communication between you and your child. Whether you're searching for the world's largest geological pothole or identifying a non-native plant such as buckthorn, this is a wonderful opportunity for you to educate and inspire in your child a consciousness about the natural world. Also included for each trail is a fun list of trivia questions. Look them over before the hike, and then answer the questions on the way home if you like.

Attached to the book's back cover is a kid's companion handbook that contains the scavenger hunt checklist (the same checklist that appears with pictures in the main book). As your child locates each item on the trail, he/she can check it off the list. If you need more copies of the handbook, either for another child or for yourself (wink), feel free to download them from the Adventure Publications' website (www.adventurepublications.net/hikingMN). Another goodie for kids is the magnifying ruler. Use it to examine insects and leaves, or measure fat, fuzzy caterpillars.

Most importantly: have fun! Spending time in the great outdoors, enjoying nature with your child is a gift of well-being that will last a lifetime.

BEFORE YOU HIT THE TRAILS

Kids are kids. They jump and climb. The right footgear is an important consideration for avoiding unnecessary accidents and injuries. But do your kids really need expensive hiking boots? That depends on how much hiking you plan to do with your kids and on what type of terrain. For most hikes, a well-fitting, good-gripping tennis shoe will be fine. But for those hard-scramble trails loaded with rocks and roots, you may want to invest in a pair of hiking boots. Boots have better ankle support and traction, as well as some water resistance. Whether you decide on tennis shoes or boots, grip and fit are the two most important features. Never let your kids hike in smooth-soled shoes! They do not provide enough traction and become slippery when wet.

Whatever kind of hiking you do, to ensure a successful outing, you'll want to make sure you pack a few necessities:

- Pack a good first aid kit for treating bug bites, burns, scrapes and mishaps. (See page 136 for first aid resources.)
- Keep your cell phone with you in case of injuries requiring medical attention (but remember that cell phones don't always work in the woods). If you don't have a cell phone, make sure you know before your hike where the nearest phone is—nature centers and campsites usually have one.
- Kids get crabby when they are hungry or thirsty, so pack plenty of water for the trail and simple snacks such as apples, grapes, granola, etc.

Kids tumble and poke their fingers where they don't belong. It would be silly to assume that you'll never encounter anything annoying or potentially harmful on the trails. Minnesota hosts such things as noxious plants, insects, ticks and two (rare) species of poisonous snakes. Some you might never meet; others will seem to be everywhere you go. The best things you can do are to be aware of your surroundings, use common sense and take practical precautions. Tips and expert-recommended suggestions for handling emergencies can be found on pages 136–141.

Take your time on the trail. The hikes are meant to be a fun and educational activity you can enjoy with your children. They are not tests of endurance. Let the kids determine the pace.

- Minnesota was admitted to the Union on May 11, 1858 as the 32nd state.

- **STATE CAPITAL**—St. Paul

- **STATE BIRD**—Common Loon

- **STATE FISH**—Walleye

- **STATE INSECT**—Monarch butterfly

- **STATE MUFFIN**—Blueberry

- **STATE TREE**—Norway Pine

- **STATE FLOWER**—Showy Lady's Slipper

- **STATE SONG**—"Hail! Minnesota"

- **STATE MINERAL**—Lake Superior agate

- **STATE MOTTO**—L'Etoile du Nord (The Star of the North)

- **STATE NICKNAME**—The Gopher State

- **STATE DRINK**—Milk

- **STATE GRAIN**—Wild rice

- **STATE MUSHROOM**—Morel

- **STATE INVENTIONS**—the black box flight recorder, cheerleading, cello-phane transparent tape, the home thermostat, the seat belt, the stapler, water skis, in-line skates, armored cars, the pop-up toaster, Scotchgard, Wheaties cereal, Bisquick, HMOs, the bundt pan, Spam, Green Giant vegetables, and Aveda beauty products.

- The nation's first open heart surgery and bone marrow transplants were per-formed in Minnesota at the Mayo Clinic in Rochester.

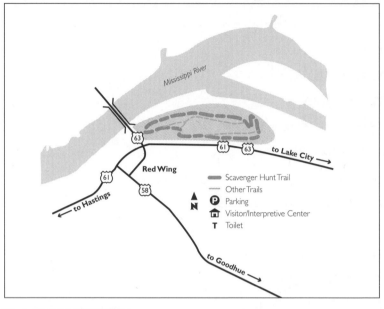

BARN BLUFF

POINTS OF INTEREST:
Old limestone kiln, city overlook, scenic river view

TOTAL TRAIL MILES: 3.5
THIS HIKE: 2 miles
DIFFICULTY: Moderate
ELEVATION: 300 feet

Officially christened by the French as Mount La Grange, Barn Bluff was once an island in a shallow sea and is over a half-billion years old. The carving force of receding glaciers are responsible for the Bluff's present form which measures roughly 3,100 feet long, 800 feet wide and over 300 feet above the river. It's been a watchtower, burial site and trading post for the Dakota Indians, a fortress of defense for early settlers, mined of limestone for more than 40 years and a source of inspiration and beauty. It is one of the most climbed bluffs in southeastern Minnesota claiming foot traffic from the likes of Henry David Thoreau, Stephen Long, Henry Schoolcraft and Henry Lewis.

Barn Bluff has 3.5 miles of trails with an elevation gain of 300 feet. The two major ones loop the bluff in a 2-mile hike. The North Trail cuts through a hardwood forest leading to an amazing scenic overlook of Red Wing and the Mississippi Valley. The South Trail is an open stroll through waist-high prairie grass. When you're through hiking the bluff, head for the backside of the underground water tank to the Kiln Trail. The road leads straight to several abandoned 1800s kilns and quarries.

WHERE TO BEGIN

Even though Barn Bluff is one of the most immediately visible and imposing structures in the Red Wing area, the trailhead is still a bit tricky to find. From Hwy 61 S in downtown Red Wing, take a right on Hwy 58 which is also Plum Street. Take a left on 5th Street and follow it all the way to the Hwy 61 underpass (dead end). Go through the underpass and park; the steps to the bluff trailhead are on the left next to a large underground water tank.

The trails are moderate in difficulty. For those with young children, Barn Bluff is one stairway after another followed by narrow dirt paths and more stairs. No shelter, restrooms or drinking water available so plan accordingly.

THE TRAILS

North Trail The incredibly scenic, fairly difficult 1-mile North Trail wraps the bluff along the riverside. It winds through a picturesque hardwood forest of sugar maples and is a gorgeous hike no matter the season, but especially so in the fall. However, this is not the trail for those who hate heights, are not mountain-goat-sure on their feet or small children under 4 years of age. If you take the kids, hang onto them, as there aren't any guardrails and it's pretty much a quick trip straight to the bottom. In many areas the trail is nothing more than a steep, very narrow (12 inches), very slick footpath hugging tight to the hillside with lots of boulders and downed trees to crawl over, under and around. It's an adventure for sure, but the river view and scenic vistas are well worth the price of a few scrapes.

Prairie Trail The 0.5-mile oak savanna prairie trail cuts straight across the top of the bluff. The overlook provides a panoramic view of Lake Pepin and the backwaters of the Mississippi. This is a fairly easy trail to navigate with children, once you make it past the trailhead steps.

South Trail The easy 1-mile trail starts out as part of the Prairie Trail with its waist-high grasses, then veers to the right and follows along the bluff edge. There are some really nice views of Red Wing's older residential neighborhoods and Sorin's Bluff, which is directly across from Barn Bluff. As far as safety goes, the trail is clear and wide, but does offer some side paths for the adventurous who want a bird's-eye view of the town. If you're concerned your kids might get too adventurous, steer them toward the short

Midland Trail found at about the halfway point on the South Trail. It stays well inland and leads to the trailhead steps.

G. A. Carlson Lime Kiln Trail Once you've hiked the bluff, head around the back side of the water tank to a gravel road marking the 550-foot Kiln Trail. The abandoned kilns and quarries are a fascinating glimpse into local history. Notice the bright white rocks strewn throughout the area—they are remnants of the kiln-fired quick lime.

SCAVENGER HUNT (North/South Trail)

1. Underground water tank and trailhead

2. Buckthorn—a vigorously growing, non-native plant.

3. Iron eye anchor

4. Rock with star drill holes

5. Original 1929 Kiwanis Stairway

6. Flag on top of the grain elevator

7. Sumac (turns bright red in the fall)

8. Old limestone kiln

9. Kiln-fired lime rock. Notice how much lighter and whiter it is from all other rocks in the area.

TRIVIA QUESTIONS

Q: What does "Mount La Grange" mean?

It's French for "twin mountain," loosely translated to "barn mountain."

Q: How high is Barn Bluff?

Barn Bluff is 334 feet above the river.

Q: Is Buckthorn a native plant to the area?

No. Buckthorn entered the United States from Europe as hedge material. This vigorous plant grows as tall as a tree. It's a real ecological threat because the chemical it secretes chokes out native plants. It's overtaking many Midwestern wilderness areas at an alarming rate.

Q: How hot were the wood fires in the lime kilns?

The wood fires in the kilns burned at 2,000 degrees Fahrenheit.

Q: What was limestone used for in 1908?

Limestone was used in the construction of buildings, bridges, riprap for the railroad, basements and walls.

THINGS TO DO IN THE AREA

Cannon Valley Rail-Trail, trailhead is one block off Hwy 61 on Old West Main and Bench Street. The picturesque Cannon Valley Rail-Trail meanders over several streams, stretching almost 20 miles from Red Wing to Cannon Falls; Welch Village is the midpoint. A canopy of trees shades nearly the entire paved trail, which is fairly level and an easy hike/bike for kids. Expect to see turtles and snakes sunning on rocks and not-quite-so-shy white-tailed deer. There are portable restrooms along the way, as well as benches for resting. Pack a picnic lunch or stop midway in Welch at the Trout Scream Café (651-388-7494) or Cannon River Inn (651-388-2057) for a bite to eat and an ice cream cone. There is a trail use fee or "wheelpass" for everyone ages 18 and up (no fee for hiking). The parking lot at the Red Wing trailhead has a primitive restroom.

Welch Mill, Cty 7, Welch; 651-388-9857. As long as you're in Welch, why not make a day of it floating on the Cannon River? Rent an inner tube, canoe, or kayak at the Welch Mill. Rental price includes life jackets, paddles and shuttle service. Open daily Memorial Day–Labor Day. Choose between 5-mile or 12-mile canoe trips.

Colvill Park, located along the Mississippi River southeast of downtown Red Wing on Hwy 61 (watch for signs); 651-385-3674. Colvill Park is always a kid favorite. There's lots to do here—picnic, playground equipment, horseshoe pits, boat launch, basketball and tennis courts, gardens. Colvill Aquatic Center boasts two 3-story slides, a zero depth area with slide for small children, diving board with life guards on duty, concession stand, sand play area and free lockers (bring your own locks). Open daily, June–Labor Day, free admission for non-swimmers; 651-388-9234.

Bay Point Park on Levee Street (head west behind the St. James Hotel), Red Wing. Watch a barge maneuver one of the sharpest turns on the Mississippi River at Bay Point Park. The park is also home to the Boathouse Village, one of the last remaining examples of a "gin pole" system. Boathouses adjust to the different water levels by riding up and down on poles.

DINING

Lily's Coffee House, 419 W 3rd Street, Red Wing; 651-388-8797. Soups, design-your-own sandwiches, baked goods; gift items; dine in or alfresco. Open year-round. Braschler's Bakery & Coffee Shop, 410 W 3rd Street, Red Wing; 651-388-1589. Soups, design-your-own sandwiches, baked goods, lunch specials. Open year-round. Blue Moon, 427 W 3rd Street, Red Wing; 651-385-5799. Homemade soups, design-your-own sandwiches, baked goods; gift items; live music on weekend evenings. Open year-round.

LODGING

AmericInn Motel, 1819 W Main Street, Red Wing; 651-385-9060. Indoor pool, adjacent to the Bierstube Restaurant (burgers and bowling lanes, game room) and near Godfather's Pizza. Best Western Quiet House, 752 Withers Harbor Dr, Red Wing; 651-388-1577. Indoor pool, next door to Perkins Restaurant. Days Inn, Hwys 61 & 63 S, Red Wing; 651-388-3568. Indoor pool and free continental breakfast. Rodeway Inn, 235 Withers Harbor Dr, Red Wing; 651-388-1502. Indoor pool, free continental breakfast, adjacent to the Bierstube Restaurant. Super 8 Motel, 232 Withers Harbor Dr, Red Wing; 651-388-0491. Indoor pool and adjacent to the Bierstube.

CAMPING

Island Camping & Marina, 2361 Hallquist Ave, Red Wing; 715-792-2502. 50 campsites with electricity, 72-slip marina on the Mississippi River, playground, hiking, fishing. Hay Creek Valley, 6 miles south of town on Hwy 58, Red Wing; 651-388-3998. 100 campsites with electricity, tent area, heated pool, playground, volleyball, horseshoes, fishing, camp store, restaurant/bar. Hay Creek is adjacent to the Richard J. Dorer Memorial Hardwood Forest with 25 miles of hiking/horse trails and an excellent trout stream. Extra fee to camp with your horse. Hidden Valley, 27172 144th Avenue Way, Welch; 651-258-4550. 200 water and electric hookups and tent area. The campground is across the bridge on the right side, along the Cannon River and the Cannon Valley Rail-Trail.

MORE STUFF

Red Wing Chamber of Commerce, 439 Main Street, Red Wing 55066; 651-388-4719. Red Wing Parks, PO Box 34, Red Wing; 651-385-3674. The Route, 1932 Old West Main Street, Red Wing; 651-388-1082; www.theroute.net. Bike rental, repairs, kayak and canoe rental. Open daily spring–fall; shorter winter hours. Evergreen Cinema 8, Red Wing Shopping Center, Tyler Rd N; 651-385-8855.

Rock with star drill holes

5 miles west of Caledonia; 507-724-2107

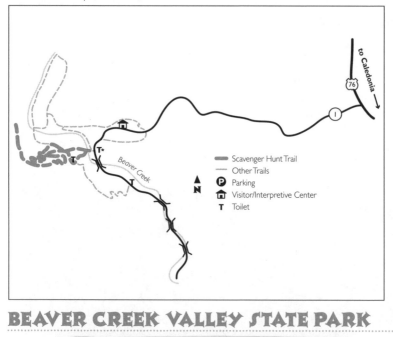

▬▬▬	Scavenger Hunt Trail
― ―	Other Trails
Ⓟ	Parking
🏠	Visitor/Interpretive Center
T	Toilet

BEAVER CREEK VALLEY STATE PARK

POINTS OF INTEREST:
Suspension bridge, spectacular overlooks, nearby 1876 Schech's Mill

TOTAL TRAIL MILES: 8
THIS HIKE: 1.25 miles
DIFFICULTY: Moderate
ELEVATION: 250 feet

The main focal point of the park is, of course, Beaver Creek. The babbling brook winds through the park's 1,187 acres and is the perfect habitat for natural brown trout (not stocked), as well as some uncommon birds such as the Louisiana Waterthrush and the rare Acadian Flycatcher. The creek is fed by numerous 47 degree Fahrenheit freshwater springs that seep from the porous valley walls, the largest of which is Big Spring.

Beaver Creek Valley State Park has 8 miles of trails with an elevation gain of 250 feet. The Switch Back Trail winds steeply upward over a spring and through a hardwood forest.

WHERE TO BEGIN

From Caledonia and Hwy 44, take Hwy 76 northwest for 2 miles (watch for park sign), then drive west on Cty 1 another 2 miles. The 8 miles of trails range in difficulty from easy along the creek to moderate bluff climbs. Park in the lot and head across the suspension footbridge for easy access to many popular trails. There is a restroom area here with drinking water. The other restroom is near the campground.

THE TRAILS

Switch Back Trail Chosen for its two beautiful overlooks, the 1.25-mile (round-trip) Switch Back Trail could be a challenge for young children, as it is mostly a steep uphill climb. The trail is paved beyond the suspension bridge up to the picnic shelter, but things get rugged once you cross the second small brook. However, the stairs keep the climb manageable for most. There are a few places where the trail deteriorates to not much more than a foot-wide dirt path, but overall it is very picturesque and the overlooks of the river valley are well worth the effort.

Once at the top, so many unadvertised trails branch from the main one that it's tough to tell which to follow. A left turn leads to one of the overlooks and a right turn leads to a short hike to the other rock outcropping, which is the overlook. All other trails travel the ridge.

SCAVENGER HUNT (Switch Back Trail)

1. Swinging footbridge over Beaver Creek

2. Wild parsnip

3. Mossy cement circle

4. Leaves with caterpillar trails

5. 500-million-year-old dolomite bedrock ledge

TRIVIA QUESTIONS

Q: Wild parsnip is a poisonous plant. Do not touch it because it can cause a nasty sunburn and rash. What should you do if you've been exposed to wild parsnip?

If you have been exposed to wild parsnip, wash your skin as soon as possible with soap and water.

Q: Big Spring is the main source for East Beaver Creek. How cold is the water coming from Big Spring?

The water flowing from Big Spring is a constant 47 degrees Fahrenheit.

Q: Beaver Creek Valley State Park and much of southeastern Minnesota is known as the "driftless area." What does that mean?

Over 10,000 years ago, glaciers covered much of Minnesota and the surrounding states. The massive walls of ice sheered off hills and leveled a lot of land. Most of it is farmland now. The glaciers did not reach Beaver Creek Valley. However, as they melted, a huge volume of extremely fast-moving water cut through the land, carving the deep river valleys you now see in this region.

Q: Beaver Creek Valley is home to an animal rare to Minnesota. What is it?

The timber rattlesnake is a rare species found in Minnesota. It is timid and poses little or no threat if you leave it alone. It is protected wildlife. If you see one, tell the park ranger.

Q: Name at least five animals you might see on a Beaver Creek Valley trail.

Animals you might see in Beaver Creek Valley include: deer, squirrels, raccoons, woodchucks, beavers, coyotes, wild turkeys, grouse, timber rattlesnakes, chipmunks, muskrats, mink, badgers and fox.

THINGS TO DO IN THE AREA

Schech's Mill, traveling northwest on Hwy 10, take a left on W Beaver Rd, then an immediate left on Mill Rd; 507-896-3481. Schech's Mill is the state's only operating water-powered gristmill with original equipment. Built in 1876, the 3-story limestone structure has been owned and operated by a member of the Schech family for three generations. No longer used for commercial flour milling, the owners give tours of the mill on weekend afternoons Apr–Oct. Small admission charged; call for tour times.

Houston Nature Center, 215 W Plum Street (eastern end of the Root River Trail, 1 block north of Hwys 16 & 76), Houston 55943; 507-896-HOOT. This is a cool new nature and information center with hands-on displays featuring a woodpecker's tongue and shrew's teeth. You can also hike the restored marsh next to the center, but the main attraction is Alice, the Great Horned Owl. Alice was permanently injured when she fell from the nest at three weeks old. She makes frequent visits to the center; call for scheduled times. Open daily.

DINING

Farmhouse Eatery & Gifts, 219 N Kingston, Caledonia; 507-725-8581. The Farmhouse Eatery is a gorgeous 1920 home with original woodwork and hardwood floors. The second floor gift shop has a nice selection of children's toys. Menu changes daily. Soups, sandwiches, desserts, root beer floats. Open Mon–Sat. Redwood Café, across from the Kwik Trip on Hwy 44, Caledonia. Known for their breakfasts, Redwood Café is a local hangout, which always means good food at good prices. Open daily at 5:30am.

LODGING

AmericInn, 508 N Kruckow Ave, Caledonia 55921; 800-634-3444 or 507-725-8000. Indoor pool, free continental breakfast, kids ages 12 and under stay free with parents. Red Carpet Inn, 15944 Hwy 76, Caledonia; 800-845-0904. Free continental breakfast.

CAMPING

Beaver Creek Valley State Park, 15954 Cty 1, Caledonia 55921; 507-724-2107. 26 campsites with electricity, 22 tent sites, a group camp and a camper cabin with electricity. Picnic grounds, large shelter with fireplace, playground equipment, volleyball and fishing. Open year-round. DunRomin' Park Campground, 12757 DunRomin' Dr, Caledonia; 507-724-2514; www.dun-rominpark.com. Large campground with hookups and primitive sites. Organized daily activities such as hay rides, kids' games, arts & crafts and nature walks. Heated pool, game room in century-old barn, 18-hole mini golf, movies, volleyball, horseshoes, trout fishing, berry picking and theme weekends, ie: barn dance, sweet corn feed, music festivals, Hawaiian night. Want to try camping, but don't have a camper? You can rent one at DunRomin' Park. Money Creek Haven, 18502 Cty 26, Houston 55943; 507-896-3544; www.moneycreekhaven.com. Electric hookups and tent sites. Pool, game room, camp store, horseshoes, volleyball, hiking, biking and restaurant with a full menu that is open daily at 5am. Supersaw Valley Campground, 22885 Cty 19 (6 miles north of Spring Grove off Hwy 4), Spring Grove 55974; 507-498-5880; www.supersawvalleycampground.com. Campsites with hookups and tent sites. Pool, 18-hole mini golf, 4 miles of hiking trails, fishing, horseshoes, basketball, volleyball, game room. Open May–Sept.

MORE STUFF

Caledonia Chamber of Commerce, 103 N Ramsey, Caledonia 55921; 877-439-4893 or 507-725-5477; www.caledoniamn.com. Houston Chamber of Commerce, P.O. Box 3, Houston 55943; 507-896-4668. Houston is the eastern trailhead for the Root River Trail. Geneva's Hideaway, (off Hwy 16), Peterson; 877-727-4816 or 507-875-7733; www.genevashideaway.com. Canoe and tube rentals. Ice cream parlor serves sandwiches, shakes, cones. Overnight rooms for rent include full kitchens.

West of the Twin Cities near Victoria; 763-694-7650

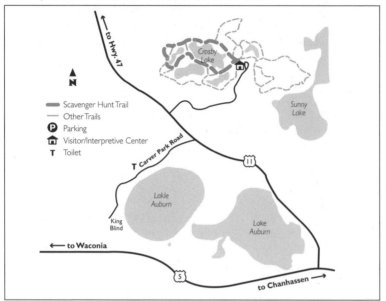

CARVER PARK RESERVE-LOWRY NATURE CENTER

POINTS OF INTEREST:
Tamarack swamp, Trumpeter Swans, nature center, butterfly garden, cool playground area, wildflower garden

TOTAL TRAIL MILES: 8
THIS HIKE: 2-mile loop
DIFFICULTY: Easy
ELEVATION: Not a factor

The Lowry Nature Center is in the middle of the 3,719-acre Carver Park Reserve—a unique ecosystem that supports forest, grassland and wetland communities. The reserve is home to the world's largest water bird—the Trumpeter Swan. Watch the graceful white birds swim across the lakes, family in tow. Many trails head toward the water's edge for just such a treat. The Fred E. King Blind on Lunsten Lake allows an unobstructed view of the swans as they do a little fishing for their dinner.

Another park resident throughout the summer months is the Osprey. Carver Park Reserve boasts the highest density of these raptors in the metro area.

The park has 8 miles of trails with an elevation gain of around 40 feet. The wide, grassy trails are gently rolling with tours around lakes, through meadows, woods and wetlands. Boardwalks allow for hikes directly through the marshes. Kids of all ages will enjoy exploring every nook and cranny of this park.

WHERE TO BEGIN

From I-494, take Hwy 5 east to Victoria; go through town and turn right on Cty 11 north (turn by the Dairy Queen), drive 1.5 miles; the park entrance is on the right.

Begin your hike at the Lowry Nature Center. The awesome prairie-style center is geared for kids with interesting year-round programs led by their full-time naturalists. Pick up a map and a bit of advice from the staff on what's happening on the trails for the day. The center also has restrooms with sink step stools for the youngsters, drinking water and a comfy seating area around a fireplace. They are open daily, year-round. Free admission.

As you head outdoors, you might lose the kids immediately at the Habitat area. This ingenious playground features equipment shaped like flowers, a beaver dam and a "dead" tree slide riddled with woodpecker holes. Surrounding the area are various animal tracks set in cement, providing the opportunity for a little detective work. How many animals can you match with their footprints? Adjacent to the playground is a wildflower garden. Down the trail a few steps is the remarkable butterfly garden with interpretive signs and walking paths.

THE TRAILS

Lake and Tamarack Trails The easy 2-mile grassy loop follows the Crosby Lake perimeter with a short jaunt through a woods and the tamarack swamp. The boardwalk through the swamp puts you at ground level with frogs, colorful wildflowers and insects and the 10-foot-tall cattails for a very cool, jungle-like adventure. Trails lead down to the lake for a close-up view of wildlife, including swans, cranes, Osprey and deer.

Cattail and Maple Trails The easy 1.25-mile loop treks through a deep maple forest and includes a nice overlook across the marsh, another cool boardwalk among the cattails and a shot at viewing an Osprey nesting site on Sunny Lake.

SCAVENGER HUNT (Lake and Tamarack Trails)

1. Tepee
2. Bluebird house
3. Butterfly gardens
4. Bog boardwalk
5. Cattails
6. Ripe cattails
7. Monarch butterfly
8. Great Egret

TRIVIA QUESTIONS

Q: What is the largest aquatic bird in the world?

The world's largest water bird is the Trumpeter Swan.

Q: What is a habitat?

A habitat is a place where plants and animals live together. Many habitats together form a community.

Q: How many communities are found at the Carver Park Reserve?

Carver Park Reserve has three communities: forest, grassland and wetland.

Q: What are the four stages a butterfly goes through to become an adult?

Butterflies are first an egg, then larva, a chrysalis and, finally, a full-fledged adult butterfly.

Q: Tamaracks are different than other pine trees because they shed their needles in the fall after they turn a beautiful golden color. The tamarack swamp in the Carver Nature Reserve is one of the few metro areas where these trees grow. However, in recent years many of these unique trees have died. Do you know why?

The swamp is getting too dry for the tamaracks.

THINGS TO DO IN THE AREA

Gale Woods Farm, 7210 Cty 110 W (from I-494, drive west on I-394/Hwy12 for 4 miles; exit on Cty 15 west in Wayzata and drive 8 miles, turn left on Cty 110, then drive 3 miles; watch for signs), Minnetrista; 763-694-2001; www.gale-woodsfarm.org. The 410-acre park houses a real working farm complete with cattle, sheep, chickens, hay fields, pastures, an orchard and vegetable gardens. Let the kids run wild with the sheep, search for eggs in the barn, learn veterinarian skills or harvest vegetables from the gardens. Produce, eggs, meat, maple syrup and honey are all grown and sold at the farm. Make a scarf from the wool spun from the farm's three breeds of sheep; the yarn comes in 30 colors for the choosing. Hayrides, picnics, fishing, hiking and canoeing make Gale Woods a great place to learn about farming and nature. The visitor center is open year-round. Park grounds are open 5am–sunset. Free barn tours on Sundays, Jun–Aug. Canoe rental available. Free admission to the park; minimal fees for programs.

Lake Minnetonka Regional Park, 4610 Cty 44 (from I-494, take Hwy 7 west for 12 miles; turn right on Cty 44 and follow signs), Minnetrista; 952-474-4822. Whether it's hot outside or not, Lake Minnetonka Regional Park is a kid favorite. And it just might have something to do with the 20,000-square-foot, nautical-themed playground and 1.75-acre swimming pond. The crystal clear water is only 6 feet deep max, with a lifeguard on duty. A bathhouse, concessions and beach umbrellas make this a favorite place for adults as well. The park also features a cool nature center, 2.5 miles of paved bike/hike trails and a fishing pier. Admission to the pond is $1/person.

Minnesota Landscape Arboretum, 3675 Arboretum Dr (9 miles west of I-494 on Hwy 5), Chanhassen; 952-443-1400; www.arboretum.umn.edu. The arboretum has over 1,000 acres of gorgeous display gardens—all designed to withstand harsh Minnesota winters. For a little taste of what's here, check out the hosta glade with its more than 300 varieties of hostas or the 150 different species of beautiful hybrid roses surrounded by fountains and trellised clematis. Some other highlights include a serene Japanese garden, a garden for wildlife and a garden guaranteed to get all of your senses tingling. The arboretum offers year-round nature programs, cooking classes, a children's garden and summer camps. It has over 12 miles of hiking/cross-country skiing trails, 3 miles of paved trails (also called the 3-mile drive for vehicles), free 2-hour guided walking tours, a tram tour ($2/person), playground equipment and picnic areas. Restrooms, drinking water, on-site restaurant (soups, salads, sandwiches), research library and a huge gift store are found in the Oswald Visitor

Center. The grounds are open daily, year-round. The visitor center is open daily year-round, but hours vary with the season. Admission charged; free for children ages 15 and under.

DINING

Piasonos Restaurant, 1550 Arboretum Blvd, Victoria; 952-443-4644. Family restaurant serves a full menu and pizza. Open year-round. Victoria House, Stieger Lake Ln (downtown, across from the lake), Victoria; 952-443-2858. Full menu with daily specials and kids' menu. Main entrance leads to lounge or family dining area. Open year-round.

LODGING

AmericInn Hotel & Suites of Chanhassen, 570 Pond Promenade; 800-634-3444 or 952-934-3888; www.americinn.com. Indoor pool and spa, free continental breakfast with waffles, adjacent restaurant and lounge. Best Western Chaska River Inn & Suites, 1 Riverbend Pl, Chaska; 952-448-7877; www.best-westernchaska.com. Indoor heated pool and spa, free continental breakfast, on-site restaurant and bar. Chanhassen Inn, 531 W 79th Street, Chanhassen; 800-242-6466; www.chaninn.com. Free breakfast, cribs and rollaways. Country Suites by Carlson, 591 W 78th Street, Chanhassen; 800-456-4000 or 952-937-2424; www.countryinns.com/chanhassen. Indoor pool and spa, free breakfast buffet with waffles, on-site lounge.

CAMPING

Lake Auburn Family Campground, Cty 11 N, Victoria; 763-559-6700; www.threeriversparkdistrict.org. 56 campsites (no electric), small sand beach (no lifeguard), nature programs, 4 lakes, fishing, hiking, biking and boating.

MORE STUFF

Chanhassen Area Chamber of Commerce, 391 W 78th Street, Chanhassen 55317-1099; 952-934-3903; www.chanhassenchamber.org. Lowry Nature Center, 7025 Victoria Dr, Victoria; 763-694-7650. Snowshoe and kicksled rentals. Three Rivers Park District, 763-559-9000; www.threeriversparkdistrict.org. Information center for 5 reserves/nature centers and camping facilities: Carver Park Reserve, Coon Rapids Dam Regional Park, Elm Creek Park Reserve, Hyland Lake Park Reserve and North Mississippi Regional Park. They also provide a list and pricing for equipment rentals and a schedule of cool, year-round nature/interactive programs fun for everyone. Grimm Farm, 763-694-7650. Tour the 1859 farmstead, considered the birthplace of all modern varieties of alfalfa—a $10 billion industry! Small admission fee. Call for tour schedule. Chanhassen Cinema, 570 Pauly Dr, Chanhassen; 952-974-1000.

Butterfly gardens

CASCADE RIVER STATE PARK

POINTS OF INTEREST:
Waterfalls, cascades

TOTAL TRAIL MILES: 18
THIS HIKE: 2 miles (round-trip)
DIFFICULTY: Easy to moderate
ELEVATION: 300 feet

On its way to Lake Superior, the Cascade River drops 120 feet in less than a quarter mile, birthing a series of gorgeous waterfalls, rapids and cascades within a twisting gorge. For the most part, the 2,865-acre state park sprawls along 5 miles of Lake Superior shoreline. Trails to Lookout and Moose Mountains and most of the river loop are on private property, so stay on the paths.

Cascade River State Park has 18 miles of hiking trails with a total elevation gain of 740 feet. The main hiking loop follows the Cascade River for a stunning view of the multiple cascades, high overlooks, valley creeks and picturesque forest.

WHERE TO BEGIN

From Tofte, drive northeast 21 miles on Hwy 61. The park entrance is on the left. Pick up a trail map at the park office, then continue driving to the campground area, which is one big loop. Instead of going into the campground, take a right at the intersection and follow to a parking lot. The trailhead to the cascades is here and so is an outdoor restroom. No drinking water other than the pump in the campground, so plan accordingly.

THE TRAILS

Cascade River Trail This 2-mile (round-trip) hike is only a portion of the actual trail. It follows the river and the beautiful cascades up to the "96 steps" mark. At this point, you can take the staircase down to the river's edge or continue farther upriver. The Spur Trail leads to a small waterfall (not running the day we were there). The Spur Trail is only 0.3 miles and scenic enough to warrant the time if you have it, but not recommended for young children. There are areas where it is incredibly steep with a path not much wider than what a mountain goat requires. The main trail is rough in areas, reduced to roots and rocks, but overall it's a great adventure most kids will love. There are ample opportunities to wade in the river as side trails abound. Benches take advantage of scenic overlooks, but exercise caution as you won't find a guardrail anywhere.

The Cascade River Trail is actually a 7.7-mile loop of the Superior Hiking Trail, as it travels from the Lake Superior shoreline along the river and into the woods on it's way to Cty Rd 45 and back again. This is a full day of sometimes strenuous hiking and not a trail for most kids. It hangs fairly close to the river, at least close enough to hear it nearly all of the time and stays true to the lay of the land. which means it gets clutch-your-heart-for-your-next-breath steep in areas. Bridges and boardwalks in the creek valleys keep your feet dry. About 4 miles into the hike as you near the road, the trail bends toward the river for an amazing view of the valley below. Walk across the bridge on Cty 45, then loop under it to catch the return trail. Again, its an up-and-down adventure through woods and vale. Keep the river to your right. NOTE: If you plan to hike the entire 7.7 miles of the Cascade River Trail, ask for the **Cascade River Loop Trail** map. This is a different map than the regular state park version.

Lake Superior Shoreline This 1-mile easy hike along the shore is fun for kids of all ages. Waves crash. Gulls dip and soar along the beach looking for food. The kids will love hunting for agates. There's an outdoor restroom by the picnic area. The parking lot is about a mile south of the park entrance on Hwy 61.

SCAVENGER HUNT (Cascade River Trail)

1. Cascades

2. Tree cages

3. Root trail

4. Blueberry bushes

5. Split rock along river

6. Birch tree

TRIVIA QUESTIONS

Q. Why do some small trees have cages around them?

Foresters put cages around seedlings to protect them from nibbling deer and other animals.

Q: Notice the peeling bark on the birch trees. What happens if you peel the bark from the trees?

Birch trees die when their bark is stripped. Centuries ago, Native Americans used the birch bark to make canoes and many different containers. They were very careful when they peeled the bark from the tree, taking only the very outer layer.

Q: How big is Lake Superior?

Lake Superior covers 31,700 square miles and holds 3 quadrillion gallons of water. That's enough to cover North and South America with 1 foot of water. It contains 10 percent of the world's surface fresh water.

Q: What is the average water temperature of Lake Superior?

The average water temperature of Lake Superior is 40 degrees Fahrenheit. Its bays can warm up to 70 degrees Fahrenheit.

Q: How many streams flow into Cascade River State Park and drain into Lake Superior?

There are 10 streams within the park.

THINGS TO DO IN THE AREA

Lutsen Mountains Recreation Area, PO Box 129, Lutsen; 218-663-7281; www.lutsen.com. There's so much to do at Lutsen Mountains and that's during the off season! Lutsen is a top-rated ski resort during the winter, but there's just as much activity throughout the summer months as well—horseback riding, mountain biking, hiking, alpine slide and tram rides. Enjoy the Sawtooth Mountains on horseback. Homestead Stables offers 1-hour trail rides, lunch rides and steak dinner rides. Open daily mid-May–Oct. You must be age 7 or older, at least 54 inches tall and weigh less than 250 pounds. Children under age 10 must be accompanied by an adult. Maybe you'd rather explore the mountains a bit closer to the ground? Lutsen has over 20 miles of bike trails ranging from easy gravel surfaces to the challenging and steep rock and dirt paths. Use the Mystery Mountain lifts to get from trail to trail. Bike rentals and lift passes available. Lutsen has over 15 miles of hiking trails. The Vasque Hiking Center provides top-notch equipment rentals such as boots, walking sticks and child carriers. Maybe you're too close to the ground and want an bird's-eye view of the area? Then hop a ride on the Mountain Tram to the highest point on the North Shore where you'll enjoy breathtaking 100-mile views. Rides are free for kids 6 and under with a paid adult. For a thrill ride, head over to the Alpine Slide. Ride the lift up the half-mile sled track, then scream your way to the bottom. Fee charged; open daily Jun–mid-Oct. NOTE: Lutsen Mountain dining opportunities abound. You may choose from deli sandwiches and ice cream to pubs to fancy-schmancy lakeside affairs.

Cascade Lodge Evening Canoe Trips, 3719 W Hwy 61 (near Cascade State Park), Lutsen; 800-322-9543 or 218-387-1112; www.cascadelodgemn.com. Take a canoe trip with the kids. Cascade Lodge supplies the canoe, equipment and guide. Tuesday evenings during July and August. Fee charged. NOTE: Cascade Lodge is a resort with log cabins, a main lodge with a family restaurant and a year-round naturalist on staff.

DINING

Mountain Top Deli, located at Lutsen Mountains; 218-663-7281. Snacks, lunch and ice cream at the summit of the Lutsen Mountain Tram. Lockport Marketplace & Deli, located at Lutsen Mountains, 218-663-7548. Open since 1928, the deli and family grill serve breakfast and lunch. Espresso bar.

LODGING

Caribou Highlands Lodge, 371 Ski Hill Rd, Lutsen; 800-642-6036 or 218-633-7241; www.caribouhighlands.com. Luxury resort with mountain and Lake Superior views. Golf, tennis, hiking, biking, skiing, pools & spas. Naturalist and children's programs. On-site restaurant, gift shop, deli and bakery. Open year-round. Lutsen Resort, PO Box 9, Lutsen; 800-258-8736 or 218-663-7212; www.lutsenresort.com. Scandinavian lodge, on-site restaurants and pubs, pool and spa, game room, shuffleboard, hiking, biking, golfing, skiing, kayaking, horseback riding, alpine slide and tram rides. Free kids' programs. Open year-round.

CAMPING

Cascade River State Park, 3481 W Hwy 61, Lutsen; 218-387-3053. 40 campsites (no electric), 5 carry-in, 2 group campsites, fishing, hiking and picnic areas.

MORE STUFF

Lutsen-Tofte Visitor Information Center, 7136 W Hwy 61 (located inside the North Shore Commercial Fishing Museum at the Hwy 61 & Sawbill Trl intersection), Tofte; 888-61NORTH; www.61north.com. North Shore information plus trail maps for the 200-mile Superior Mountain Bike Trail System. Homestead Stables, Lutsen Mountains Recreation Area; 218-663-7281; www.lutsen.com. Horseback trail rides: 1-hour lunch or dinner rides. Lutsen Mountains Recreation Area, PO Box 129, Lutsen; 218-663-7281; www.lutsen.com. Bike rentals, bike park, tram, alpine slide, skiing. Gitchi Gami Bike Trail, www.ggta.org.

Root trail

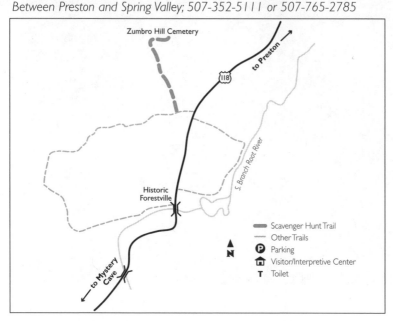

FORESTVILLE/MYSTERY CAVE STATE PARK

POINTS OF INTEREST:
Historic 1899 Forestville, Carnegie Steel Bridge, pioneer cemetery

TOTAL TRAIL MILES: 16
THIS HIKE: 0.5 mile
DIFFICULTY: Easy
ELEVATION: 220 feet

In 1850, Levi Waterman staked his claim to Forestville by carving his name in an oak tree. Waterman later sold the land to Robert Foster, who enticed his brother-in-law Felix Meighen to move to Forestville and join him in the venture. In its heyday, Forestville was a bustling town of 150 people, boasting two hotels, a general store, brickyard, school, distillery, two sawmills, a gristmill, cabinet shop, blacksmith shop and post office. However, when the railroad decided to bypass the town, many of the people and businesses moved to larger, more prosperous communities. By 1890, the Meighen General Store was the last remaining business in town. Meighen closed up shop in 1910, leaving everything preserved exactly as it was.

Today, thanks to the Minnesota Historical Society's efforts, Forestville continues on as a living history museum. Costumed interpreters take on the tasks of the 1899 residents running the general store, tending to the housework, cooking on a wood burning stove, gardening, grinding feed for the chickens with a hand grinder, fanning oats and making tools by hand. They are a fun and knowledge-able bunch who love help with their chores like feeding the chickens, gathering eggs and making axe handles, but "modern" devices such as cameras and cell phones draw a lot of questions from them. Enter the town via the Carnegie Steel Bridge, which was the last structure built in Forestville and thought to be the oldest remaining bridge in Fillmore County. Open daily Memorial Day–Labor Day, closed on Mondays. Open weekends only in September and October. Fee charged, but admission is free for children ages 5 and under. Restrooms, drinking water and a gift shop are found in the visitor center. The park also features picnic areas, campsites, trout fishing, snowmobiling and cross-country skiing.

NOTE: Due to the constant battle with state budget shortfalls, hours of opera-tion may vary from year to year; call ahead for current hours.

WHERE TO BEGIN

The Forestville/Mystery Cave Park entrance is 4 miles south of Hwy 16 on Cty 5, then 2 miles east on Cty 118 in Fillmore County.

The 2,000-acre Forestville State Park is the most heavily used horse camp in the state and a paradise for bird watchers, as it is home to the rare Louisiana Waterthrush. It also features sinkholes, blue ribbon trout streams and skunk cabbage (which smells like something died). Skunk cabbage is found the first part of March on the Fern Loop. There are 16 miles of hiking trails varying in difficulty from easy to moderate. No restrooms and drinking water on the trails.

THE TRAILS

Cemetery Trail The 1-mile (round-trip) trail is an easy hike up 220 feet under a gorgeous canopy of maples and savanna oaks. The trail ends in the middle of an 1850s pioneer cemetery and according to the site manager Sandy Scheevel, many children make charcoal etchings of the tombstones. Although it's a bit steep, the trail is about 8 feet wide and graveled. An added bonus of this hike is there are no side trails for little ones to run off on. Find the trailhead 1 mile from Historic Forestville on Hwy 118. It is on the left side immediately after the dry gully and just past the brown wood park signs. The schoolhouse site is about 50 feet beyond the trailhead by the metal yellow park sign.

Big Spring Trail The beautiful 3-mile (round-trip) Big Spring Trail treks along the Canfield Creek. It crosses the stream twice without the aid of a bridge, so you will need to wade through the 48-degree water. On a hot day, mist shrouds the trail due to the temperature difference between the air and the water. The hike ends at a 200-foot-high limestone bluff, the source of the spring-fed creek. An unadvertised trail winds up to the top of the bluff. Moderate in difficulty, this is a great hike for adventurous kids, but not recommended for young children. Begin the hike near the group campsite, head south and take the stairs to the iron bridge.

Sinkhole Ridge Trail The 3-mile Sinkhole Ridge loop offers a great sunset view. Watch for sinkholes on the east side. Fillmore County has more than 6,000 sinkholes because its rock base is primarily karst, a fractured limestone. There's only 5–10 inches of topsoil, so when it rains the soil slowly seeps into the cracks in the limestone, causing sinkholes. The trail has an elevation gain of 200 feet and follows the ridge east of town. It's an easy hike.

NOTE: The nearby town of Fountain is the self-proclaimed "Sinkhole Capitol of the U.S." Have a look at one of their sinkholes located at a wayside stop 4 miles north of Preston on Hwy 52.

SCAVENGER HUNT (Cemetery Trail)

1. Remains of the 1880 two-story Forestville "Graded" School

2. Brick from the 1855 Brickyard site

3. Horseshoe on the hitching post

4. Coral fungi found on rotting logs (not poisonous)

5. "Troll-face" tree growth

6. Headstone in Pioneer Cemetery

TRIVIA QUESTIONS

Q: Who owned the entire town of Forestville in 1899?

Thomas Meighen was the owner of Forestville in 1899. All 50 residents worked for him on his farm or in his store.

Q: What was the most popular item sold in the Meighen General Store?

Chewing tobacco was the store's most popular item. Boys started "chewing" at age 13.

Q: In 1899, how much money were people paid for their work?

In 1899, men earned $1 a day and women earned 42 cents a day. House rent was $3 a month. People could rent a cow for 50 cents a month.

Q: How old were children when they graduated from "graded" school?

Children entered school in grade "G" and graduated after finishing grade "A," usually around the age of 13. There were seven lettered grades.

Q: The Meighen General Store is one of the oldest buildings in Minnesota. The bricks used to build it were made in a Forestville brickyard. How did they make the bricks?

Clay and water were used to make the bricks used in the construction of the Forestville buildings. Workers dug clay from the hillside and mixed it with water from the stream. The mixture was molded in wooden forms and left to dry. Once dry, the bricks were put in a very hot oven called a kiln. This process made them hard enough to use for houses and other buildings.

THINGS TO DO IN THE AREA

Mystery Cave, PO Box 128 (5 miles south of Historic Forestville off Cty 5), Preston; 507-937-3251; www.dnr.state.mn.us. Explore Mystery Cave—Minnesota's longest cave with more than 13 miles of passages. The 1-hour, half-mile guided tour marches through two levels of fossils, crystal clear pools, curtains, stalactites and stalagmites. Concrete ramps make the tour stroller friendly. The temperature is a constant 48 degrees Fahrenheit and damp, so dress accordingly. Open daily Memorial Day–Labor Day; weekends only May, Sept, Oct. Fee charged, but admission is free for children ages 4 and under.

Niagara Cave, Drive 2 miles south of Harmony on Hwy 139, then 2 miles west on Niagara Cave Rd (about 23 miles from Mystery Cave); 800-837-6606 or 507-886-6606; www.niagaracave.com. With its 130-foot-high ceilings, pitted limestone passageways and 60-foot waterfall, Niagara Cave is the Grand Canyon of the underground. This is a fun and interesting hour-long guided tour the whole family will enjoy. Wear comfortable shoes and bundle up as the cave is a chilly 48 degrees Fahrenheit. Open daily Memorial Day–Labor Day; weekends only April, May, Sept, Oct. Admission charged; free for children ages 3 and under.

Root River/Harmony-Preston Valley Trails (bike/hike), Historic Bluff Country, Inc., 15 2nd Street NW, PO Box 609, Harmony; 888-223-4258; www.bluff-country.com (free visitor guide). Sixty-six miles of paved trail from Houston to Fountain (east to west) and Isinours to Harmony (north to south), with 61 picturesque bridges, make the Root River/Harmony-Preston Trails the area's number one attraction and one of the most popular recreational trails in the United States. Bike, in-line skate, or hike the former 1860 railway as it meanders alongside the magnificent Root River and limestone bluffs. You'll see plenty of deer, wild turkey and hawks. No use fees except for cross-country skiing.

Trolley Tours, Tours & Treasures, 102 E Beacon Street (located in the restored 1890 Feed Mill), Lanesboro; 866-349-4466 or 507-467-4466. Ride Molly the Trolley on a 1-hour narrated tour through Historic Lanesboro, the agricultural countryside and the DNR state fish hatchery. Daily tours (weather permitting) mid-March–Oct. Fee charged.

Amish Tours. Over 100 Amish families make their home in southern Minnesota. It is the largest Amish population in the state. Take the kids on a tour for a glimpse into life before electricity and cable TV. There are several Amish tours available; most stop at farms, drive by schools and take in some historic sights like the 1856 restored Lenora Stone Church. For tour information see the More Stuff section in this chapter.

Amish Buggy Ride, Gator Greens, 439 Half Street (Hwy 16 & Cty 36), Whalan; 507-467-3000. Here's a chance to view the world as the Amish do with a 30-minute buggy ride that seats four. It is an interesting tour of Whalan and some of the surrounding countryside. Tours given Wed–Sat at Gator Greens. Fee charged.

DINING

Aroma Pie Shoppe, 618 Main Street, Whalan; 507-467-2623. Billed as "Home of World Famous Pies," Aroma Pie Shoppe is a must stop for anyone who believes "nothin says lovin" quite like fresh pie from the oven. They have all the favorites like apple, banana cream, lemon meringue, pecan and strawberry (in season). They also serve Belgian waffles with fresh strawberries and whip cream every morning from 8–11am. Bridgeman's Ice Cream, malts, floats, turnovers, muffins, cinnamon rolls, cookies, cakes and more. They have a great sandwich selection, salads, soups and "Little Tykes Sandwiches" for children ages 1 to 9 (American cheese grilled on white bread or peanut butter and jelly, also on white bread with kettle chips, pickle and cookie nuggets). Located on the Root River Trail. The Riverside on the Root Restaurant/Deli, S Parkway Ave, Lanesboro; 507-467-3663. The restaurant overlooks the Root River and the old railroad trestle bridge. Eat indoors or out on the patio. Open daily. Full menu includes pizza, pasta, subs, walleye, prime rib, elk tenderloin. Live music on Wednesday and Sunday evenings. River Trail Picnic Basket, 100 Parkway Ave N, Lanesboro; 507-467-3551. Located on the trail, they have great smoothies, sandwiches, gourmet coffees and 16 flavors of Bridgeman's ice cream—how does it get better than that? Open daily, summer season.

Rhino's Pizza & Sub Shoppe, 111 Parkway Ave N, Lanesboro; 507-467-2200. Homemade pizza, subs and sandwiches, broasted chicken, salads, soft-serve ice cream and a kids' menu. Open daily. **Das Wurst Haus German Village & Deli**, 117 Parkway Ave N (across the street from the bike trail), Lanesboro; 507-467-2902. For the more adventurous kids, try the Das Wurst Haus home-made sausages, meats, cheese, breads, soups and sauerkraut. They also have homemade root beer, fudge, Amish candy and ice cream. Listen to the live polka band or take your sausage to go and grill out in Lanesboro's **Sylvan Park**, also found on the main drag in town. The park has a nice pavilion, grills and playground equipment. Das Wurst Haus German Village & Deli is open daily. **The Brick House on Main Coffeehouse**, 104 E Main, Preston; 507-765-9820. Located 3 blocks from the Preston Root River trailhead. Smoothies, root beer floats, Chai, gourmet coffees, pastries, soups, sandwiches. Open year-round. **Village Square**, 51 Main Ave N, Harmony; 507-886-4406. Pizza, sandwiches, burgers, salads, homemade pies, cookies, ice cream, kids' menu. Look for the red and white stripped awning.

LODGING

Country Trails Inn, 809 Hwy 52, Preston 55965; 888-378-2896 or 507-765-2533; www.countrytrailsinn.com. Indoor pool and spa, free continental breakfast and located on the Preston Root River trailhead. **Cedar Valley Resort**, 905 Bench, Whalan 55949; 507-467-9000; www.cedarvalleyresort.com. Six deluxe log cabins from 1,400 to 2,500 square feet, on 30 picturesque acres. They are equipped with everything you need including a gas fireplace and full kitchen. Also lots to do in the way of entertainment: Frisbee golf, horseshoes, sand volleyball, badminton, croquet and bocce ball. Rentals include bike, tube, canoe and kayak. **Country Lodge Motel**, 525 Main Ave N, Harmony; 800-870-1710 or 507-886-2515. Located in the midst of Amish Country, the Country Lodge Motel in Harmony is close to all the tour action, plus the state park and Root River Trail. Free buffet breakfast—and this is quite a breakfast—lumberjack quantity and quality. Kids ages 12 and under stay free with their parents.

CAMPING

Forestville/Mystery Cave State Park, located 4 miles south of Hwy 16 on Cty 5, then 2 miles east on Cty 118 in Fillmore County; 507-352-5111 or 866-857-2757; www.stayatmnparks.com. 73 campsites (23 electric), horseback riders campground has 60 units (23 with electricity), 16 miles of hiking/horse trails, some of the state's best trout fishing, cave tours and historic Forestville tours. **Maple Springs Campground and Country Store**, located on a century-old farm on Cty 118 (a couple miles before Forestville State Park entrance); 507-352-2056 or 507-886-2410; www.maplespringscampground.com. 69 campsites, both electrical/water hookups and primitive. Nature trails, fishing, camp store, located near the state park. Open April–October. **Amish Country Camping**, I mile east of Harmony on Hwy 52 (watch for sign), Harmony; 507-886-6731. Enjoy primitive camping on an Angora goat farm. Take a free farm tour. Help owner Ada Austin feed her goats and three rare Navajo-Churro sheep. Gift shop, camp store, nearby cave and Amish tours, portable restrooms. **Lake Louise State Park**, located 1.5 miles north of LeRoy on Cty 14 (766th Ave), LeRoy, 507-324-5249. 22 campsites (11 electric), 6 horse campsites. Hiking and horse trails, paved bike trail, fishing, small nature store, picnic shelter and swimming beach. **Eagle Cliff Campground and Lodging**, located on the Root River 3 miles east of Lanesboro on Hwy 16; 507-467-2598; www.eaglecliff-campground.com. 120 campsites with electric hookup, 55 tent sites and a motel. Eagle Cliff is close to the Root River Trail. They have canoe, kayak, tube and bike rentals. **The Old Barn Resort & River's Bend Golf**, 4 miles west of Lanesboro; 800-552-2512 or 507-467-2512; www.barnresort.com. The 200-acre campground and hostel is located on the Root River Trail. Heated indoor pool, fishing, 18-hole golf and driving range, basketball, horseshoes, volleyball, bar & grill (open daily mid-April–October at 11am), 40 primitive and 130 campsites with electricity. **Sylvan Park & Riverview Campgrounds**, Parkway Ave S, Lanesboro; 507-467-3722. 43 campsites with electricity, 60 more tent sites. Nice city park with picnic area, grills and playground equipment.

MORE STUFF

Lanesboro Area Chamber of Commerce, 100 Milwaukee Road, PO Box 348, Lanesboro; 800-944-2670 or 507-467-2696; www.lanesboro.com. **Historic Bluff Country Regional Convention & Visitors Bureau**, 800-428-2030 or 507-886-2230; www.bluffcountry.com. **Root River Outfitters**, S Parkway Ave (main street across from The Red Hotel), Lanesboro; 507-467-3400; www.rootriver-outfitters.com. Canoe, tube and bike rentals. Open daily Memorial Day–Labor Day; weekends only Sept and Oct. **Little River General Store**, 105 Coffee Street, Lanesboro; 800-994-2943 or 507-467-2943; www.lrgeneralstore.com. Canoe, kayak and bike rentals. No rental tubes, but you can buy one for $40. They also sell and repair bikes. **Gator Greens Mini Golf & More**, 439 Half Street (Hwy 16 & Cty 36), Whalan; 507-467-3000; www.GatorGreens.net. 9-hole mini golf course, tube and kayak rentals. **Horse-drawn carriage rides** Wed–Sat. Ride leaves from 102 Beacon Street, Lanesboro; fee charged, children 5 and under are free if they ride on adult's lap. Call ahead for a reservation 507-467-7000; www.ggcarriages.net. **Amish Country Tours**, 800-278-8327 or 507-886-2303; www.shawcorp.com/amish. **Amish Tours of Harmony**, 45 Main Ave N, Harmony; 800-75-AMISH or 507-886-5392; www.bluffcountry.com/amish.htm. Open year-round, Mon–Sat. **R & M Amish Tours**, R. 2, Box 202, Lanesboro; 507-467-2128 (day) or 507-467-3040 (eve.); www.rmamish.com. Open year-round, Mon–Sat. Tours run Apr–Oct. **Flaby's**

Amish Tours, PO Box 277, Lanesboro; 800-944-0099; http://flaby.tripod.com. Apr–mid-Nov. Commonweal Theatre, 206 Parkway Ave N, Lanesboro; 800-657-7025 or 507-467-2525; www.commonwealtheatre.org. Performances Feb–Dec. Call for production schedule and ticket price. Bluff Country Jeep Tours, 111 1st Street, Whalan; 507-467-2415 or 507-467-2388. Open Apr–Oct. Back roads trek through the hills and valleys near Whalan. Lanesboro State Fish Hatchery, RR 2, Box 85, Lanesboro; 507-467-3771. Free tours. Open Mon–Fri. Root River Adventures Unlimited, Jeff Olson & Jack Currie, PO Box 14, Rushford; 507-467-2231. Fishing guides for Trout and Small Mouth Bass. May–Sept. Avian Acres, Norway Dr (1½ miles southwest of Lanesboro; follow signs); 800-967-2473 or 507-467-2996; www.aawildbirdsupply.com. Avian Acres specializes in wild bird supplies, but also has a petting zoo with over 100 animals including deer, pygmy goats and miniature donkeys. Open year-round Tues–Sat.

Northeast of Two Harbors on Hwy 61; 218-834-3855

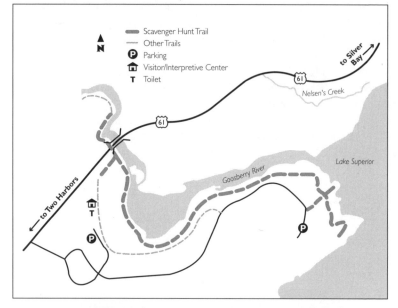

GOOSEBERRY FALLS STATE PARK

POINTS OF INTEREST:
Five waterfalls, nature center

TOTAL TRAIL MILES: 18
THIS HIKE: 2 miles
DIFFICULTY: Easy
ELEVATION: 175 feet

Established in 1937, Gooseberry Falls is Minnesota's most popular state park with nearly 1 million visitors annually. What do they come to see? Waterfalls, waterfalls, waterfalls. The Gooseberry River plunges over a series of five, 30-foot-high waterfalls on its way to Lake Superior.

The 1,662-acre park has 18 miles of trails with an elevation gain of 175 feet. None of the trails are especially difficult to navigate, but there are stairs, some rooty and rocky terrain, lots of rushing water (in spring being the wildest) and steep drop-offs and no guardrails, so keep young children in hand.

WHERE TO BEGIN

From Two Harbors, drive northeast about 13 miles on Hwy 61. The park entrance is on the right. Begin your hike with a tour of the fabulous nature center. Exhibits showcase native plants and animals. A short movie provides interesting facts about the Great Lakes. The nature center also has restrooms, drinking water and a large gift shop. The trails straight out from the nature center are paved, and many have benches strategically placed for spectacular views. Gooseberry Falls has a year-round naturalist program.

THE TRAILS

River View Trail The 2-mile (round-trip) trek begins at the nature center and travels downriver to the shores of Lake Superior, where you'll find an agate beach, nice picnic shelter with fireplace and restrooms with drinking water. The trail hugs fairly tight to the river with fabulous views of the middle and lower falls, but eventually veers into a swamp that features a bountiful crop of snake root before climbing out of the bog and toward the lake. About halfway into the hike there is an opportunity to cross a footbridge and head back to the Middle and Lower Falls, or you can take the connecting Gitchi Gummi Trail. The highlight of the 1-mile loop is a rocky ledge lookout of Lake Superior, but again, keep a good eye on the young ones as it is a drop of at least 100 feet straight down. For the return trip, take the bike trail back to the nature center. This trail follows the river ridge through the woods to Gateway Plaza, where you'll discover a sculpture that was a hinge pin and truss segment from the original 1925 Gooseberry River Bridge. Lots of interesting information here as well about the history of the Gooseberry Falls region. Continuing onward under the bridge, the Upper Falls is only a short distance farther.

Fifth Falls Trail The short 1.5-mile loop is steeper, rockier and more rugged than the River View Trail. The trail links with the Superior Hiking Trail and runs along both sides of the river, connected by a footbridge at the falls. Access the trailhead at the Hwy 61 bridge and head upriver.

SCAVENGER HUNT (River View Trail)

1. Waterfalls

2. Cave

3. Raspberry bush

4. Part of the original 1925 river bridge

5. Gooseberry bush

6. Footbridge

7. Snake plant

TRIVIA QUESTIONS

Q: How did Gooseberry Falls get its name?

No one is positive how Gooseberry Falls got its name, but there are two stories. The Ojibwa Indians called the area "Shabonimikani-siba," which means "the place of the gooseberry." If you look around, you'll notice the park does have a lot of gooseberry bushes. Another possibility is the river was named after the French explorer, Medard Chouar des Groseilliers, whose last name "Groseilliers" means "gooseberries."

Q: The Ojibwa Indians used to harvest needles from Balsam Fir trees year-round. What did they use the needles for?

The Ojibwa used the balsam needles to make tea.

Q: The Ojibwa harvested the bark from the Paper Birch tree. How did they use the bark?

The Ojibwa used the birch bark as an outside covering for their homes. They also made bowls, canoes, baskets and household storage containers from the bark.

Q: Why is the river water the color of root beer?

The river begins in a wetland area. When the plants die and decay, they release acids that run into the water and color it brown.

Q: What are the top 10 things kids like to do in Gooseberry Park?

1. Visit the interpretive center, 2. Buy souvenirs, 3. Camp, 4. See the water, 5. Hike, 6. Fish, 7. Cross-country ski, 8. Snowshoe, 9. Sightsee and 10. Go to nature programs.

THINGS TO DO IN THE AREA

Two Harbors Waterfront. Head to the waterfront in Two Harbors for a look at the historic 1896 Edna G. Tugboat, one of the oldest steam-powered tugs to serve the area. Two Harbors still welcomes its share of large lake carriers throughout the summer months. More than 10 million tons of ore are shipped from this port annually. You can watch as they load the 1,000-foot-long carriers with taconite.

Split Rock Lighthouse, 3713 Split Rock Lighthouse Rd, Two Harbors; 888-727-8386 or 218-226-6372. Built in 1910 atop a 130-foot-high, 2-billion-year-old cliff, Split Rock Lighthouse commands an awesome Lake Superior view. Costumed guides take you through the keeper's home and to the top of the lighthouse tower for a look at the Fresnel lens. The interactive history center teaches through interesting exhibits and videos about the sailing dangers posed by the lake and the challenging lighthouse construction. Built long before Hwy 61 existed, all materials had to be shipped in, then hoisted or hauled up the cliff. Daily tours mid-May–mid-Oct. Call for winter hours. Admission charged.

Superior Hiking Trail, 731 7th Ave, PO Box 4, Two Harbors 55616; 218-834-2700; www.shta.org. According to *Backpacker* magazine, the Superior Hiking Trail is the second best long-distance trail in the nation and it consistently ranks as one of the top 25 hikes in the world. The trail is a rugged 235-mile jaunt through thick hardwood forests and river valleys. It begins just north of Two Harbors and travels along the North Shore all the way to the Canadian border. It links seven state parks, three state waysides, several state forests and the Superior National Forest. Unparalleled scenery includes towering vistas of Lake Superior, waterfalls and cascades galore, 300-foot-high palisades and lush, nearly tropical flora. The trail is well built and well marked, but challenging. Lots and lots of steep climbs and rocky or rootbound paths. However, for those who truly love a "nice walk in the woods," the Superior Hiking Trail is a hiker's paradise. There are 29 different trailheads—several are accessed off Hwy 61. Park your vehicle at one of the entrances, then arrange to be picked up at the end of your hike by Superior Shuttle, located at 2618 Hwy 61 E, Two Harbors; 218-834-5511 or 612-803-8453. They'll even give your pets a ride!

DINING

Betty's Pies, 2 miles north of Two Harbors on Hwy 61; 877-269-7494 or 218-834-3367; www.bettyspies.com. With more than 50 kinds of freshly baked pies, it's tough to make a decision. (Go for the Five Layer Chocolate!) Homemade breads also baked daily. Sheer willpower is the only thing that will get you out of the place and back to your hiking. Open daily, year-round; breakfast, lunch and dinner. **Do North Pizzeria,** 15 Waterfront Dr, Two

Harbors; 218-834-3555. Red or white sauce pizza. Open daily. **Vanilla Bean Bakery & Cafe**, 812 7th Ave (Hwy 61), Two Harbors; 218-834-6964 or 218-834-3714. Sandwiches, baked goods, soups, salads, pizza. Open daily, breakfast, lunch and dinner. **Rustic Inn Cafe and Gifts**, 2773 Hwy 61 (near Gooseberry Falls State Park), Two Harbors; 218-834-2488. Built in the 1920s, the Rustic Inn Cafe has a full menu, cappuccino, ice cream, homemade fudge and pie. All-day breakfast, lunch and dinner. Large gift shop. Open daily, year-round.

LODGING

AmericInn Lodge & Suites, 1088 Hwy 61 N, Two Harbors; 800-634-3444 or 218-834-3000; www.americinn.com. Indoor pool and spa. Free continental breakfast. **Country Inn Two Harbors**, 1204 7th Ave, Two Harbors; 218-834-5557; www.countryinntwoharbors.com. Indoor pool and spa, free continental breakfast. **Grand Superior Lodge on Lake Superior**, 2826 Hwy 61, Two Harbors; 800-627-9565 or 218-834-3796; www.grandsuperior.com. Main lodge has a pool and spa, on-site restaurant, lounge and gift shop. Rooms, log homes or cabins available. **Lighthouse Bed & Breakfast Inn**, 888-832-5606 or 218-834-4814; www.lighthousebb.org. The 1892 lighthouse is Minnesota's oldest operating light station and also a bed and breakfast. This is your chance to be a real keeper as the guests take care of the lighthouse duties during their stay. What a cool way for kids to be a part of history! **Superior Shores Resort & Conference Center**, 10 Superior Shores (Hwy 61), Two Harbors; 800-242-1988 or 218-834-5671; www.superiorshores.com. Indoor and outdoor pools, on-site restaurant and lounge.

CAMPING

Gooseberry Falls State Park, 3206 Hwy 61, Two Harbors; 218-834-3855. 70 campsites with electricity and 3 group campsites. Trout fishing, hiking, biking and year-round naturalist program. **Knife River Campground**, 196 Scenic Dr, Knife River; 218-834-5044; www.kniferivercampground.com. 25 campsites (some electric), playground. **Split Rock Lighthouse State Park**, 2010A Hwy 61, Two Harbors; 218-226-3065. 24 primitive tent campsites (all walk-in only). Fishing, hiking, biking and visitor center with a lighthouse.

MORE STUFF

Two Harbors Area Chamber of Commerce, 1026 7th Ave, Two Harbors; 800-777-7384 or 218-834-2600; www.twoharborschamber.com. **Superior Shuttle Service**, 2618 Hwy 61 E, Two Harbors; 218-834-5511 or 612-803-8453; www.superiorshuttle.com. Shuttle service for man and (small) beast to and from the Superior Hiking Trail. Operates Fri, Sat, Sun, mid-May–mid-Oct. **Beaver Bay Sport Shop**, Hwy 61 E, Beaver Bay; 218-226-4666; www.beaverbaysports.com. ATV rentals, 3-hour minimum. Snowmobile rentals and guide service available. **Lake Superior Charter Fishing**, PO Box 81, Two Harbors; 218-854-4270; www.fishduluth.com/rainbowsend. **Silver Creek Sled Dogs**, PO Box 309, Two Harbors; 218-834-6592. Dog sled mushing. Variety of trips range from 30-minute rides to overnight camping tours.

Footbridge

On Hwy 61 at the Canadian/U.S. border; 218-475-2360

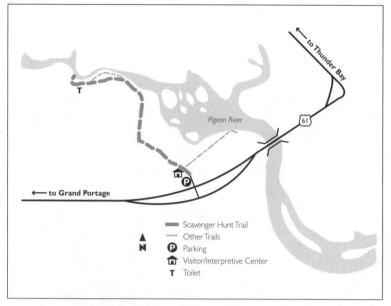

GRAND PORTAGE STATE PARK

POINTS OF INTEREST:
The 120-foot High Falls, Middle Falls,
flume remnants, Canada

TOTAL TRAIL MILES: 5

THIS HIKE: 1 mile

DIFFICULTY: Easy

ELEVATION: 300 feet

Divided by the Pigeon River, Minnesota shares its highest falls with Canada. The 300-acre Grand Portage State Park is actually not owned by Minnesota, but by the local band of Chippewa Indians and maintained primarily by the DNR. The lower 20 miles of the river is a chain of rapids, waterfalls and gorges impossible for boat navigation. To get around these obstacles, the early Native Americans developed a 9-mile trek inland called the Grand Portage, or "the great carrying place." For centuries, this was the only way for people such as those in the fur trade and timber industries to reach interior destinations.

Grand Portage State Park has 5 miles of trails with an elevation gain of 300 feet. The trail to the High Falls is easy with wide grassy paths and a boardwalk. The Middle Falls trail is challenging and not recommended for young children.

WHERE TO BEGIN

Grand Portage is at the very tip of the Arrowhead region. Take Hwy 61 northeast as far as you can go without crossing the Canadian border; the entrance is on the left. The park office has a small gift shop and trail maps. You can also pick up trail maps at the Grand Portage Bay Information Center located a few miles south of the park on Hwy 61.

Grand Portage has an outdoor restroom and picnic area near the parking lot and another located before the boardwalk. No drinking water, so plan accordingly. This is a day-use state park—no camping allowed.

THE TRAILS

High Falls Trail The 1-mile (round-trip) grassy path through the hardwood and birch tree forest changes to a boardwalk through the wettest part of the trail. It's pretty easy going for most of the hike until the scenic overlook of the falls, where you'll find a set of stairs. The view of the 120-foot High Falls is nothing short of thrilling. Look for the rainbow in the mist at the bottom of the falls. On the Canadian side of the Pigeon River, notice the remains of the flume leftover from the logging era. Bikes are prohibited on this trail, but strollers are fine. Most of the steep cliff areas and overlooks have some sort of guardrail or wall protection, with the exception of the unadvertised goat paths branching from the main trail. Return to the parking lot via the same route.

Middle Falls Trail The 3.5-mile trail is a rugged, sometimes difficult climb over ridge tops and through the forest. It offers breathtaking views of the river gorge and Lake Superior, but no conveniences such as restrooms. The 20-foot-high Middle Falls is a nice payoff for your labor, but this is truly northern back country and not recommended for young children. For the return trip, double back the same way you came, or follow the river on the 1-mile Middle Falls Loop through spruce, birch and aspen. Some of the trail is still under construction, so talk to the ranger about hiking conditions before setting out.

SCAVENGER HUNT (High Falls Trail)

1. Moss-
   covered logs

2. Bug foam

3. High Falls

4. Remains of 1899 log flume

TRIVIA QUESTIONS

Q: The Pigeon River serves as the borderline for what two countries?

The United States and Canada are separated by the Pigeon River.

Q: How did loggers get the logs over the falls without damaging them?

In 1899, the loggers constructed a flume to bypass the falls and send the logs on their way down the river to the sawmills on Lake Superior.

Q: What is the "Grand Portage?"

The Grand Portage is a 9-mile trail the Indians created to get around the river's 20 miles of waterfalls and rapids. It was also used by voyageurs and fur traders, who carried their canoe and at least 90-pounds of supplies and furs on their backs for the entire 9 miles. Grand Portage means "the great carrying place."

Q: What did the early voyageurs use for bug repellent?

The voyageurs used bear grease and skunk oil to keep mosquitoes away. It probably kept everyone else away, too-pugh!

Q: The High Falls are at least 120 feet high. They are Minnesota's highest falls. How much water goes over the falls?

Around 3,200 gallons plunge over the High Falls every single second.

THINGS TO DO IN THE AREA

Grand Portage National Monument, 1 mile south of Hwy 61 on the Grand Portage Indian Reservation (7 miles south of the Canadian border; watch for signs on Hwy 61); 218-475-2202 or 218-387-2788; www.nps.gov/grpo/home1.htm. The 9-mile Grand Portage trail linked Lake Superior and Montreal with westward systems of lake, rivers and interior trading posts. Established in 1731, the village of Grand Portage was the state's first white settlement and the largest fur-trading depot on the continent. The stockade, great hall and kitchen have been reconstructed on the original sites. Costumed interpreters demonstrate birch bark canoe making, musket firing, adobe oven bread baking—everything a busy eighteenth-century fur trader may have encountered while hanging out at the fort.

Several hiking trails branch from the monument. The Mount Rose paved trail is a steep 1-mile (round-trip) climb up catwalks and steps to a scenic overlook of the fort and Lake Superior. Trails and monument grounds are open year-round; buildings open daily, mid-May–Oct. Bookstore, interpretive exhibits, displays, videos, picnic area, restrooms and drinking water. Small fee charged.

Isle Royale Excursions, Grand Portage; 888-746-2305 or 715-392-2100; www.grand-isle-royale.com. At 45 miles long and 8 miles wide, Isle Royale is the largest in a chain of Michigan islands stretching 50 miles across Lake Superior. Native American copper miners settled Isle Royale long before Columbus sailed the ocean blue. Take the kids on an island day trip. See a 400-year-old tree, a lighthouse and a sunken steamship. Fish, hike, canoe, kayak, camp or stay at the Rock Harbor Lodge. Scenic cruises depart May–October. Boats have restrooms and concessions; no pets allowed on the island. Fee charged; free for children ages 3 and under. Purchase tickets at the dock or in advance by calling 888-746-2305.

DINING

Grand Portage Lodge & Casino, 70 Casino Dr, Grand Portage; 800-543-1384 or 218-475-2476; www.grandportage.com. Restaurant with full menu; separate lounge. Open daily, year-round. Ryden's Border Café/Phillips 66 & Convenience Store, ½ mile south of the Canadian border on Hwy 61; 218-475-2330. Souvenir shop, restaurant, gas and currency exchange.

LODGING

Grand Portage Lodge & Casino, 70 Casino Dr, Grand Portage; 800-543-1384 or 218-475-2476; www.grandportage.com. Pool and spa, casino, on-site restaurant and store. Hollow Rock Resort, 7422 E Hwy 61 (3 miles south of Grand Portage), Hovland; 218-475-2272; www.hollowrockresort.com. Cabins next to the water. Two motel rooms. Rock Harbor Lodge, on the northeastern end of Isle Royale; 888-746-2305 or 715-392-2100. Boat and canoe rentals. Package rates and housekeeping cottages available. NOTE: Rock Harbor serves meals for all campers and hikers in the lodge dining room.

CAMPING

Grand Portage Marina & Campground, Marina Rd (next to the Grand Portage Lodge & Casino), Grand Portage; 218-475-2476. Grand Portage National Monument, located 1 mile south of Hwy 61 on the Grand Portage Indian Reservation. This is primitive back country camping; walk-ins only. No charge, but permit required, which can be purchased at one of the three self-register boxes along the trail.

MORE STUFF

Grand Portage Bay Travel Information Center, Hwy 61; 218-475-2592. 24-hour rest/picnic area with scenic overlook. Open May–Oct. GPIR Line, Inc. (Isle Royale National Park headquarters), 1507 N 1st Street, Superior, WI 54880; 888-746-2305 or 715-392-2100.

45 miles northeast of the Twin Cities in Taylors Falls; 651-465-5711

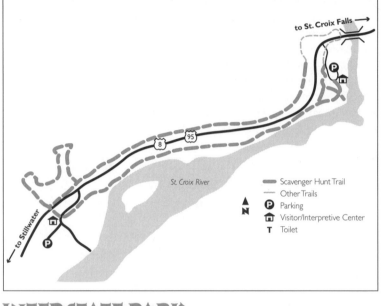

INTERSTATE PARK

POINTS OF INTEREST:
Potholes, waterfall, scenic river valley view

TOTAL TRAIL MILES: 4

THIS HIKE: 4 miles

DIFFICULTY: Moderate (easy around the potholes)

ELEVATION: 250 feet

Established in 1895, Interstate is Minnesota's second oldest state park and one of the coolest! It is the twin to the Interstate Park directly across the St. Croix River in Wisconsin. The 295-acre park features some of the world's largest and deepest potholes. Over 10,000 years ago, as the last of the glaciers melted, raging waters and silt bored perfectly round craters into the 1-billion-year-old basalt. As a result, the trail along the bluffs looks like pothole Swiss cheese! The retreating waters also carved the beautiful St. Croix valley as you see it now. The 200-foot palisades are a popular draw for rock climbers and Bald Eagles.

The park has 4 miles of trails with an elevation gain of 250 feet. The ever popular quarter-mile Pothole Trail skirts the cliffs above the river for amazing views. The main hiking loop consists of the River and Railroad Trails. The River

Trail winds in and out of the woods and along the highway, eventually joining with the wooded Railroad Trail for a total hike of 2.75 miles.

WHERE TO BEGIN

Interstate is a cinch to find. From east I-94, take the Stillwater exit onto Hwy 95. Stay on Hwy 95 north all the way to Taylors Falls. The main park entrance is to the right at the stoplight (only one stoplight in town).

Both the Pothole and River Trails begin behind the visitor center. For those with young children, beware—the Pothole Trail is treacherous. The other trails are scenic and moderate in difficulty with lots of stairs and steep climbs. No paved trails. The visitor center has interesting interpretive exhibits highlighting the region's formation, a small nature store, maps, restrooms and drinking water. There's another set of restrooms and drinking water at the south end of the River Trail, as well as maps, information, bird checklist, picnic area, canoe rentals and campground. No swimming. Interstate also has an educational craft page for kids. Ask for it at the campground information center.

THE TRAILS

Pothole Trail Not to be missed is the truly awesome 0.25-mile interpretive Pothole Trail. The numerous perfectly crafted craters look like some giant drill went berserk. The 60-foot-deep Bottomless Pit is thought to be the world's deepest pothole. The potholes would disappear without a regular cleaning of the leaves, rocks, grass and trees that take root inside them. The trail is an easy scramble over natural basalt formations. The especially high vantage offers spectacular views of the river valley and neighboring Wisconsin.

From a parent's perspective, the trail is both amazing and terrifying. Besides the 60-foot-deep potholes, the trail wanders along the steep bluffs above the river. No guardrails, so keep a sharp eye. For those with strollers, the shorter paved trail features many of the large potholes.

River Trail This is an interesting 1.25-mile hike of moderate difficulty. It travels through woods, swamp and along the highway offering memorable views of the river gorge. The trail is a variety of dirt, crushed slate, stairs and large boulders covered in lichen and moss; it is not stroller friendly. The trail ends at the campground information center; restrooms and drinking water found here.

NOTE: This trail has quite a few convincing goat paths masquerading as the real deal, but these quickly narrow and lead down to the river. As you hike south from the visitor center, the main trail veers right and is covered with crushed slate.

Railroad Trail Pick up the moderately difficult 1.5-mile Railroad Trail at the campground information center. Hike through the tunnel beneath the highway. At this junction you have two choices: continue the trail through the woods, or hike the 1-mile Sandstone Bluffs Trail. The trail leads to Curtain Falls, a mere trickle through the summer months. It loops back onto the Railroad Trail after a steep hike upward to the 500-million-year-old sandstone bluffs—the highest point in the park offering a panoramic view of the valley.

Railroad Trail continues north toward town through thick woods of sugar maples, birch, aspen, basswood and oak. There's a steep stair climb near the remains of the old railroad bridge. At the end of the trail you'll find the old depot and the oldest remaining public school in the state, est. 1852. The trail is not stroller friendly, but it's a fast moving hike with plenty of things along the way to pique a kid's interest and yours, too!

SCAVENGER HUNT (All Trails)

1. The Lily Pond

2. The Bottomless Pit

3. Heart-shaped pothole

4. Exclamation point-shaped pothole in basalt wall

5. Rock covered with lichen

6. Pointed rocks in wall

7. Animal paw print in step

8. Remains of an old railroad bridge (4 pillars)

9. Striated multicolored iron basalt. Stones carried by glaciers scraped against the hard basalt, creating scratch marks (striations).

10. Oldest existing public school in Minnesota, est. 1852

TRIVIA QUESTIONS

Q: What is the name of the deepest pothole in the world?

The deepest pothole in the world is the Bottomless Pit. It is 60 feet deep and 10 feet wide, but there is evidence some of the unexplored potholes in the park could claim the title.

Q: During the 1987 restoration, what was found in the Bottomless Pit?

The Bottomless Pit contained lots of paraphernalia from the 1940s–1950s: grape soda and Orange Crush bottles, Ol' Smoothie Root Beer bottle, buttons, comb, cup, golf ball, pipe, glasses, photos.

Q: How many potholes are in Interstate Park?

Interstate Park is home to the world's largest collection of potholes. There are at least 140 potholes in the park, with more to discover.

Q: How did the Dalles of the St. Croix form?

Over a billion years ago, earthquakes erupted and lava covered the area. The incredibly hard, dark gray basalt rock of the St. Croix valley is actually cooled lava. Basalt is the most common rock found in the earth's crust and makes up the greatest share of all ocean floors.

Q: There are a lot of lichen-covered rocks in the woods. What is lichen?

Lichen is the combination of alga and fungus. The alga and fungus need each other. The fungus creates shelter for the alga. The photosynthetic alga provides carbohydrates (food) for the fungus.

THINGS TO DO IN THE AREA

Taylors Falls Scenic Boat Tours, (next to Interstate Park); 800-447-4958 or 651-465-6315. Chug the St. Croix River aboard one of two authentic paddle-wheelers in the Taylors Falls Scenic Boat Tours fleet. The tours include interesting narratives about the river valley, plus a chance to sharpen your imagination to see what the guide sees in the various rock formations. Open May–mid-October. A choice of **7-mile or 3-mile trips** offered daily from mid-June–August. Wednesday evening **picnic cruises** board at 7pm and return at 9pm. The cost includes a narrated tour, buffet meal of baked chicken, barbecue ribs and all the trimmings. Other cruise packages available. Onboard concessions, cash bar and restrooms.

Wild River Stable, take Hwy 95 west to Almelund, then go 3 miles north on County 12. Right next to Wild River State Park; 651-583-2178. Guided horse rides through Wild River State Park for everyone from the beginner to the experienced rider. The charge is by the hour or a full day's ride. Call for details.

Wild Mountain, from the Taylors Falls stoplight, drive 5 blocks through town on the main drag to Cty 16. Turn right on Cty 16 and drive 7 miles to Wild Mountain, Taylors Falls; 800-447-4958 or 651-465-6315; www.wildmountain.com. This giant recreation park is fun for everyone. Ride a chairlift to one of two 1,700-foot Alpine slides, then curve and dip all the way back down to the bottom. The water park has slides, chutes, flume, lazy river, cargo climbing net, water cannons, hydro fountains, waterfall and zero depth area for small children. Wild Mountain also has Go-Karts and Kiddie Go-Karts, picnic areas and concessions. Wild Mountain is also one of Minnesota's top ski and snowboard destinations with 25 runs.

Scenic Osceola & St. Croix Railway, 114 Depot Rd (8 miles south of St. Croix Falls on Hwy 35), Osceola, WI; 800-711-2591, 715-755-3570 or 651-228-0263; www.mtmuseum.org. Take the kids on a ride aboard vintage steam and diesel powered trains. This is not a stuffy, museum-like trip. Costumed volunteers ride along to answer questions, but you and the kids are free to move about. Onboard bathrooms and concessions. Open weekends Memorial Day–October.

Cascade Falls, Cascade Street (main street), Osceola, WI. This is the perfect spot to cool off with the kids. Hike down the 156-step stairway and splash in the cool shallow pool below the stunning 25-foot falls. Take the footbridge across the bog and explore the woodland trails.

DINING

The Drive-In Restaurant, Hwy 95 (main drag), Taylors Falls. Get your burgers and homemade root beer served to you by bebopping carhops in poodle skirts. If you've got a classic cruiser, drive her on in and get 10 percent off the menu on Thursdays. Open mid-April–mid-October. Rocky River Bakery, 360 Bench Street, Taylors Falls; 651-465-7655. Homemade soups, design-your-own sandwiches or wraps, baked goods include kringles, pies and wild rice oatmeal bread. Open year-round Wednesday–Monday (call for hours). Schoony's Malt Shop & Pizzeria, 384 Bench Street, Taylors Falls; 651-465-3222. Great old-fashioned parlor décor to go along with the tasty old fashioned ice cream. Flavors range from kiwi to mixed berry and everything in between, including chocolate and vanilla. Schoony's is famous for their thick malts. They cost $4.50, but are worth every cent! 1919 root beer on tap, fudge shop, Coney Island hot dogs and pizza. Dine in or alfresco. Open daily April–October. Late November–December, open Thursday–Monday. Cash or check only.

LODGING

The Springs Country Inn, 361 Government Street (in town about a block from the stoplight) Taylors Falls; 800-851-4243 or 651-465-6565; www.springscountryinn.com. Not a fancy place, but clean and conveniently located to Interstate Park. The restaurant serves good food with a full menu (pizza, Mexican, steak, chicken, sandwiches, etc.) and bar. Holiday Inn Express, 2190 Hwy 8 (1.5 miles east of St. Croix River), St. Croix Falls, WI 54024; 877-422-4097 or 715-483-5775; www.hiexpress.com/stcroixvalley. Heated indoor pool, whirlpool, game room, free continental breakfast and adjacent to Embers America Family Restaurant. Wannigan Point Cabins, 150 Maple Street (go 4 blocks on Main Street, take a right on Chisago for 2 blocks, turn right on Maple) Taylors Falls; 651-465-3247; www.wanniganpoint.com. Beautiful log cabins with all the amenities: gas fireplace, fully equipped kitchen, full bath, AC, insulated, phone, cable TV, linens; crib and highchair available.

CAMPING

Interstate Park, PO Box 254, Taylors Falls, MN 55084; 651-465-5711. 37 semi-modern campsites (22 with electricity), tent area, nature store, canoe rental, 4 miles of hiking trails, rock climbing, fishing, excursion boats, glacial potholes, waterfall, visitor center. Wildwood RV-Park & Campground, PO Box 235 (from the Taylors Falls stoplight, drive west on Hwy 8 for 3 miles; campground is on the right), Taylors Falls, MN 55084; 800-447-4958 or 651-465-6315; www.wildmountain.com. Over 100 campsites with water and electricity, tent area, mini golf, hiking, heated outdoor pool, game room, playground, basketball, volleyball, horseshoes, free shuttles to Taylors Falls Canoe Rental. Open May–September.

MORE STUFF

Taylors Falls Chamber of Commerce, PO Box 238, Taylors Falls, MN 55084; 651-465-6315; www.taylorsfallschamber.org. Taylors Falls Canoe Rental, located inside Interstate Park; 800-447-4958 or 651-257-3550; www.taylorsfallscanoe.com. Open daily Memorial Day–Labor Day. Quest Canoe, 340 E Mckenny Street, St. Croix Falls, WI; 715-483-1692. Wild River Canoe Rental, 572 Bench Street, Taylors Falls; 651-257-3941. Falls Cinema 5, St. Croix Falls, WI; 715-483-1471. Adventure Falls Mini Golf (next to The Drive-In Restaurant on Hwy 95); 800-996-4448 or 651-465-6501. 18-hole course with waterfall.

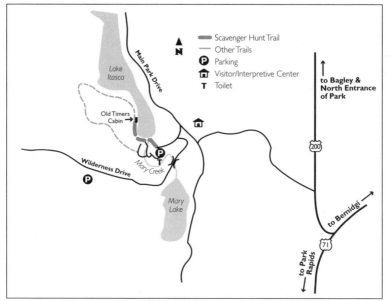

ITASCA STATE PARK

POINTS OF INTEREST:
Old Timer's Cabin, historic Douglas Lodge, visitor center,
Mississippi headwaters, Aiton Heights Tower, old sawmill

TOTAL TRAIL MILES: 33

THIS HIKE: 0.75 mile (round-trip)

DIFFICULTY: Easy

ELEVATION: Not a factor

Itasca is Minnesota's first state park. More than a half-million people visit the park annually. Established in 1891, Itasca is the celebrated birthplace of the Mississippi River, but if viewing the humble beginnings of the nation's mightiest river isn't reason enough to pack the kids into the SUV, then here are several others: the park's 49 square miles contains over 100 lakes, a very cool 100-foot lookout tower, several hands-on interpretive centers, 500-year-old Indian burial mounds, the state's biggest red pine, a pioneer cemetery and an historic sawmill.

Itasca State Park has 33 miles of picturesque hiking trails that weave through three different ecosystems, including old growth pine forests. The total elevation gain within the park is about 200 feet from Lake Itasca to the base of the lookout tower. The trails vary in length and difficulty, but most are doable for kids of all ages. The ones featured are fairly short, strictly chosen for ease and interest.

WHERE TO BEGIN

Itasca State Park has three entrances: south, east and north. The south entrance is located on Hwy 71, just 21 miles north of Park Rapids. The main east entrance is northwest of Hwy 71 on Hwy 200. Both entrances lead to the Jacob V. Brower Visitor Center. The north entrance, at the junction of Hwy 200 and Cty 2, is the fastest route to the headwaters.

The Jacob V. Brower Visitor Center is a very worthwhile stop. Brower mapped the Mississippi headwaters and became the park's first superintendent. Pick up a trail map and check out the interactive exhibit hall and 5-minute movie. Both do a nice job explaining the park's history and its three ecosystems—conifer, hardwood and prairie grassland. You'll also find a monthly schedule of all the cool naturalist programs—most are free of charge. The kids will love the fun discovery corner that was built just for them, complete with crawl-through logs and hand puppets. The visitor center is open year-round and has a gift shop, restrooms and drinking water.

THE TRAILS

Maadaadizi Trail "Maadaadizi" is the Ojibwa word for "start a journey." Located next to the Jacob V. Brower Visitor Center, the 0.5-mile Maadaadizi Trail is a great place to start your Itasca hiking journey. The level, grassy footpath is easy walking and suitable for a stroller. Interpretive signs detail the natural history of the park's forests.

Old Timer's Cabin This easy 0.75 hike is part of the Dr. Roberts Nature Trail—a 2-mile, self-guided loop that overlooks the East Arm of Lake Itasca and Lyendecker Lake. To find the trailhead, take the stairs behind Douglas Lodge to the lake, then veer left past the boat docks and fishing pier. Follow a boardwalk through the bog to the Old Timer's Cabin. The cabin is the first project built in the park by the Civilian Conservation Corps (CCC). At the time, the trees were so huge that it took only four logs to build the cabin's walls. Once the stairs to the lake have been navigated, the trail is manageable for all ages. Restrooms are near the boat dock and the Douglas Lodge area.

Historic Buildings Tour There are six historic buildings in the Douglas Lodge area; many were built during the Great Depression by the CCC. This is a very short, self-guided hike. The kids will have fun walking across the footbridge above the ravine and learning about life at the turn of the twentieth century. Free maps available at the visitor center. Several restrooms and drinking water nearby, as well as in the lodge.

Itasca Historic Sawmill The 2.25-mile (round-trip) grass path leads through a hardwood forest to what was once a busy sawmill. Antique logging equipment still sputters to life during an annual festival. The trailhead is a little tricky to find. Heading northwest toward the headwaters, you'll find a parking lot to your left (after the Wegmann Store Ruins). Park in the lot and look for the trailhead across the road (north). The hike itself is fairly level and fine for strollers, but can get a bit long for children under the age of 6, as there's little to see until reaching the sawmill. There is a restroom at the site.

Mississippi Headwaters & Schoolcraft Trail The birthplace of the mighty river is found behind the Mary Gibbs Mississippi Headwaters Center—a gift store and information center named after the brave young woman who was the nation's first female state park manager. At 24 years of age, Ms. Gibbs kept the park from flooding and killing the pines by holding her ground against the men of a logging company who threatened her at gun-point. Thanks to Ms. Gibbs' determination, the logging company opened their dam, lowering the water, which saved the trees. The actual trail to the headwaters is about 600 feet in length. A stone path leads across the great river's humble beginnings. Take the boardwalk back to the center, or hike the easy 1-mile Schoolcraft Trail, which offers a view of Lake Itasca and Schoolcraft Island. Led by the Native American guide Ozawindib, Henry Schoolcraft is the explorer credited with finding the source of the Mississippi. The center has restrooms and drinking water.

Aiton Heights Trail The 100-foot-high tower, which, by the way, is a mere 120 steps to the top, is accessed by a 1-mile (round-trip) uphill hike. Young children will find the trail strenuous, but for all else it's a gorgeous trek through hardwoods with a phenomenal panoramic payoff that includes lake views and thick forests. The view is breathtaking any time of year, but is especially so during the fall leaf season. A primitive restroom is located at the trailhead parking lot, which is southwest of the Jacob V. Bower Visitor Center off of Wilderness Drive. Note: If you happen to be visiting Itasca in the fall, note the gorgeous golden color of the tamarack trees—the only conifers to shed their needles in the fall.

Wilderness Drive & Bike Route The 15-mile paved loop circles Lake Itasca and the Wilderness Sanctuary. Some highlights include Peace Pipe Vista (a scenic overlook), "cat-faces" (triangular scarring at the tree's base caused by forest fires), the Pioneer Cemetery, the remains of the Wegmann Store and museum, the headwaters, a 300-year-old white pine, the largest red pine in the state and the Aiton Heights fire tower.

SCAVENGER HUNT (Old Timer's Cabin Trail)

1. Douglas Lodge—built in 1906

2. Original stone wall and stairs built by the CCC

3. Boardwalk through the bog

4. Wheels—the remains of a device that brought boats ashore

5. Old Timer's Cabin

6. Wood chair

7. "Cat face"

TRIVIA QUESTIONS

Q: What are the three big pines of Itasca State Park?

The three largest pines growing in Itasca are the Jack, red and white pines. The red and white pines can live for hundreds of years. In fact, Itasca is home to the state's biggest red pine. It is over 300 years old!

Q: The Old Timer's Cabin is how many logs high?

The Old Timer's Cabin was the first project in the park built by the Civilian Conservation Corp (CCC). It was built in December 1933 and is a total of four logs high. In 1933, the trees were much older and larger, as they had not yet been logged.

Q: The Ojibwa called the Mississippi "Gichiziibi." What does that mean?

The Ojibwa word "Gichiziibi" means "great river."

Q: What is a fiddlehead?

A fiddlehead is a young, sprouting fern.

Q: Plants are a source of food for microscopic and larger plant-eating animals, including us. What other important roles do plants serve?

Besides a food source, plants also provide habitat, purify water, reduce wind, stabilize soil, trap heat and eventually decompose to nutrients.

THINGS TO DO IN THE AREA

Coburn's Lake Itasca Tours, located within the park; 218-547-4150 or 218-732-5318; www.cobornscruises.com. Coburn's offers narrated boat tours to the Mississippi Headwaters. The tour traces the same 1832 route taken by Indian guide Ozawindib when he led Henry Schoolcraft to the source of the Mississippi. Open Memorial Day–September. The cruise boards by the boat docks behind Douglas Lodge. Fee charged; children ages 3 and under free with a paid adult. Buy tickets as you board. Concessions on board, but no restrooms. The closest restroom is in the Douglas Lodge, but there's also a primitive toilet near the dock. Pets are allowed only with the captain's permission.

Charlie's Ottertail Tubing, located 7 miles east of Detroit Lakes off of Hwy 34; 218-847-3258 or 218-846-1539. Go tubing on the Ottertail River. Charlie's provides free shuttle service to the river and free cooler tubes on a first-come, first-served basis. They have two rules: you must wear tennis shoes and NO glass on the river. Look for them in the big pink building.

Rising Star Ranch, located 21 miles north of Park Rapids on Hwy 71 (near the state park); 888-900-1749 or 218-266-3376. Trail rides, pony rides and a petting zoo make this a great place to take the kids. The zoo has llamas, deer, rabbits, pigs, miniature goats and buffalo. They are open daily, Memorial Day–Labor Day. One- and 2-hour trail rides. Fee charged; reservations required. Minimum age for the trail ride is 6 years.

Moondance Ranch and Adventure Park, located 5 miles south of Walker on Hwy 371; 218-547-1055; www.moondanceranch.com. Moondance is a wildlife park featuring bear, lions, deer, peacocks, timber wolves, lynx and more, but it's also a water park with waterslides and a hot tub, go-carts, mini golf, a video arcade, horseback trail rides and a restaurant. There's something here for everyone. Open daily, Memorial Day–Labor Day. Fee charged.

DINING

Douglas Lodge, located within the park; 218-266-2122. Kick back and relax at the historic Douglas Lodge. They feature Minnesota favorites such as Lake Itasca wild rice soup, wild rice hot dish, walleye, burgers and sandwiches. Dessert includes giant cookies, ice cream, cheesecake and homemade pies. Breakfast, lunch and dinner; open daily Memorial Day–mid-Oct. **Rapid River Logging Camp,** 21305 Fox Haven Trl (take Hwy 71 north from Park Rapids and follow signs to Cty 18), Park Rapids; 218-732-3444. Chicken and dressing, pork chops and ribs served family style for an authentic logging camp experience. Rustic dining hall, long pine picnic tables and tin plates and cups make you want to clad yourself in plaid and head outdoors to swing an axe. Visit the museum, petting zoo and hike the nature trails. The steam-powered sawmill runs on Tuesdays and Fridays. Open daily, Memorial Day–Labor Day. **Pizza Ranch, Lori Lea Lanes,** Hwy 34 E, Park Rapids; 218-732-4229. The Pizza Ranch serves buffet and individual pizzas, as well as sandwiches. It is connected to the bowling lanes. Open daily, year-round. **Town of Dorset,** north of Hwy 34 on Cty 226, between Akeley and Park Rapids. This small town, with a population of 22, is billed as the "restaurant capital of the world." It has more restaurants per capita than any other town in the world. Its main drag features German, Italian and Mexican cuisine. Also gift shops and ice cream shops. Some restaurants close through the winter.

LODGING

AmericInn Lodge & Suites, 1501 1st Street E, Hwy 34 E, Park Rapids; 800-634-3444 or 218-732-1234; www.americinn.com. Pool and spa, free continental breakfast. **C'Mon Inn Motel,** Hwy 34 E, Park Rapids; 218-732-1471; www.cmoninn.com. Indoor pool and spa, free continental breakfast. **Eagle Beach Resort,** 13240 Cty 40, Park Rapids; 800-284-5661 or 218-732-5050; www.eaglebeachresort.com. Sand beach on Eagle and Potato Lakes. Heated pool and wading pool, kids' activities, tennis, volleyball, baseball, putting green, paddleboats, kayaks and boat with cabin. Open mid-May–Labor Day.

CAMPING

Itasca State Park, 36750 Main Park Dr, Park Rapids; 218-266-2129 or 218-266-2100. 230 campsites (99 electric), 11 tent sites, cabins, lodge guest rooms, hostel and primitive cabin. Hiking, fishing, swimming, biking, snowshoeing, snowmobile trails. Naturalist-led interpretive programs. **Big Pines Tent & RV Park,** 501 Central Ave S, Park Rapids; 800-245-5360 or 218-732-4483. 70 campsites, some with electric hookups. Recreation hall, adjacent to the Heartland Bike Trail. Open May–Sept. **Breeze Camping Resort,** HC 05, Box 321 (9 miles north of Park Rapids on Hwy 71), Park Rapids; 218-732-5888; www.sceniclodging.com. 120 campsites (with electric), cabins and tenting on the shore of Eagle Lake. Sand lakeshore beach. Heated pool, recreational lodge with snack bar and camping supplies, volleyball, shuffleboard, horseshoes; free canoes, paddleboats and kayaks. Next to a golf course. **Long Lake Park & Campground,** 213 Main Ave N (5 miles from Itasca State Park on Hwy 200), Bagley; 218-657-2275 or 218-694-6227; www.longlakepark.com. 92 campsites, scuba diving, hiking, fishing, playgrounds, volleyball court, paddleboats, boat rentals, weekend ice cream socials. Open mid-May–mid-Sept. **Round Bay Resort & RV Park,** 23608 Hwy 87, Park Rapids; 800-231-6357 or 218-732-4880;

www.roundbay.com. 22 campsites with electric, some tent sites and cabins on Third Crow Wing Lake. Swimming, fishing, playgrounds, nature trail. Open mid-May–Sept. Spruce Hill Campground, 17404 Driftwood Ln, Park Rapids; 218-732-3292. 57 campsites on Long Lake. Swimming, fishing, playground, game room, ball fields, disc golf, camp store. Boat, motor, pontoon and canoe rentals.

MORE STUFF

Park Rapids Area Lakes Chamber of Commerce, 1204 Park Ave S, Hwy 71, Park Rapids, 56470; 800-247-0054 or 218-732-4111; www.parkrapids.com. Itasca Sports Rental, located in the park; 218-266-2150; www.itascasports.com. Bike and boat rentals (all kinds), fishing equipment and bait, boat motors. Also bike repair and camp store. Open May–mid-Oct. Heartland Bike Rental, 202220 Friar Rd, Park Rapids; 218-732-3252. Bike rental. Muskie Waters Co., 111 Bunyan Trail Rd, Nevis; 218-652-3767. Bike rental, miniature golf course, espresso, ice cream, malts, homemade desserts and gift shop. Open daily. Woodtick Musical Theater, Akeley; 800-644-6892 or 218-652-4200; www.woodticktheater.com. Live theater mid-June–mid-Sept. Kids ages 6 and under free. Long Lake Theater, 4 miles south of Park Rapids on Hwy 71, then left on Hwy 87 to Hubbard, then right on Cty 6; 218-732-0099; www.longlaketheater.net. Live theater. Jasper's Jubilee Theater, 1 mile east of Park Rapids on Hwy 34; 218-237-4333. Live comedy and music theater. Park Theatre, Main Street, Park Rapids; 218-732-3461. Movies. Green Acres Pitch & Putt, 810 Henrietta Ave, Park Rapids; 218-732-7888. 9-hole mini golf; open daily Jun–Aug. Evergreen Park, 10 miles north of Park Rapids on Hwy 71; 218-732-9609. Mini golf, go-carts, bumper boats, batting cages, the Maze, concessions. Freedom Ridge ATV Resort, 10694 Hwy 200 (17 miles north of Park Rapids); 218-732-3938. ATV and snowmobile rentals. Agri-Tourism, University of Minnesota; 877-997-2508. Call the U of M for information about the following ranch tours: Northland Bison Ranch, 877-453-9499 or 218-652-3598; www.northlandbison.com. American buffalo; fee charged; Heart of Minnesota Emu Ranch, 218-652-3790; free walking tour, 500 birds. Free admission; Double J Livestock, operating sheep ranch; Briard's Hog Farm, pigs, cattle, deer, peacocks; Jake's Syrups and Natural Products, tour of the sugar bush operation and maple syrup facility; 218-863-2508; Aho Brothers Dairy, 500 cow dairy farm.

Douglas Lodge

3 miles east of Carlton on Hwy 210; 218-384-4610

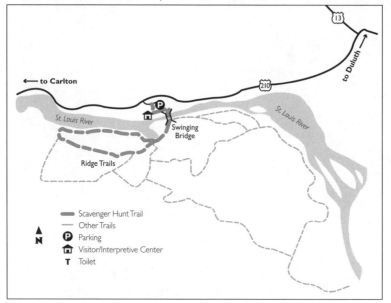

JAY COOKE STATE PARK

POINTS OF INTEREST:
Swinging bridge, St. Louis River Gorge,
Willard Munger Bike Trail

TOTAL TRAIL MILES: 50

THIS HIKE: 1 mile

DIFFICULTY: Moderate

ELEVATION: 180 feet

The 9,000-acre Jay Cooke State Park is probably most famous for its swinging bridge suspended across the indescribably beautiful and wild St. Louis River Gorge. The river roars through the area in a multitude of root beer-colored cascades on its way to Lake Superior.

Because of the park's enormous size, it is a natural habitat for more than 46 animal species including white-tailed deer, black bear, timber wolves and coyotes. There are over 16 types of snakes, but none are poisonous. Over 180 bird species such as the Great Blue Herons, Marsh Hawks and Pileated Woodpeckers nest and hunt for food in the park.

Jay Cooke State Park has 50 miles of trails with an elevation gain of 180 feet. All hikes will be a challenge for young children, with the exception of the short paved trails found in the picnic area.

WHERE TO BEGIN

Jay Cooke State Park is 10 miles southwest of Duluth. From I-35, drive east on Hwy 210 through Carlton and Thomson. The park trailhead is on the right side in the picnic area.

Begin your hike with a trip through the 1930s stone visitor center. You'll find great information here about the park and surrounding area, as well as restrooms, drinking water and interpretive programs. Two different films loop continuously: the wildflowers of Jay Cooke State Park and the 1905 construction of the Thomson Hydroelectric dam and plant (located west of the park on Hwy 210). A short, paved trail leads to the swinging bridge across the St. Louis River Gorge, but that's about as far as you'll take a stroller. Due to steep and rocky terrain, the scavenger hunt hike ranks as moderate in difficulty.

THE TRAILS

West Ridge Trail Once past the bridge, all trails become rugged routes through the woods, along the river bottom, atop the ridges and through open meadows. This hike is 1 mile of the West Ridge Trail, and it is a beauty. After the bridge, stay right. The trail travels up and down steep ravines, through a boggy wooded area and dips down along the jagged river shoreline. The trail disappears for a bit along the river. This is not a hike for young children, but those ages 6 and older should love it. There are many opportunities for scrambling onto the river rocks, depending on the water level. Notice the unusual, sharply slanted slate.

East Ridge Trail After the bridge, stay left and take the 4-mile (round-trip) trail downriver. Again, this is a rocky jaunt as it follows the rapids until it joins with the small Silver Creek. Follow the creek to the intersection named Silver Creek Trail, but head south over a footbridge. After another intersection, you'll wind up at a shelter and 60-foot-high overlook of the river valley. For a change of scenery on the return trip, backtrack to the Silver Creek Trail intersection, then head left on the trail as it parallels the creek. NOTE: Across the road from the visitor center, several trails link with the Willard Munger State Trail.

SCAVENGER HUNT (West Ridge Trail)

1. Swinging bridge

2. St. Louis River Gorge

3. Tilted rocks

4. Ripple marks imprinted on rocks from an ancient sea

5. Tree felled by beaver

TRIVIA QUESTIONS

Q: A lot of white-tailed deer live in the park. What do they eat?

Deer eat a variety of plants, but they prefer leaves, twigs and grasses. They also eat fruit, flowers, lichens, mushrooms, crops and insects.

Q: Can you name the four types of rocks found in Jay Cooke State Park?

Graywacke is a dark gray rock that shows layers of quartz. Conglomerate is a rounded pebble, brown in color. Sandstone is a sandy, reddish rock. Slate is gray and often layered.

Q: How were the rocks formed?

About 2 billion years ago, seawater covered the entire Jay Cooke region, depositing layers of mud, sand and gravel. After millions of years of heat, pressure and underground movements, the compressed rock became slate and graywacke.

Q: What caused all the rocks in the gorge to be tilted?

The underground movements that formed the rocks also caused them to buckle and fold.

Q: What is the name of the river in Jay Cooke State Park?

The river is the St. Louis. It drops nearly 500 feet in elevation as it flows through the park to Lake Superior.

THINGS TO DO IN THE AREA

Superior Whitewater Raft Tours, 950 Chestnut Ave, Carlton; 218-384-4637; www.minnesotawhitewater.com. Take a thrill ride down the St. Louis River on a Superior Whitewater Raft. They supply the gear, shuttle and experienced guides. No experience necessary, but must be age 12 or older. Trips run daily May–September. Fee charged.

Willard Munger State Trail (Carlton to Duluth), exit I-35 onto Hwy 210; drive east to Carlton; at the four-way stop, turn onto Cty 1. The trailhead parking lot is south, one block. The 14.5-mile paved bike trail from Carlton to Duluth rolls through the woods alongside Jay Cooke State Park, over a high bridge with a view of the river gorge and parallels a stream. The last 9 miles is downhill into Duluth with a stunning view of Lake Superior. The trail ends behind the Willard Munger Inn. No restrooms or drinking water along the way, so plan accordingly.

Lake Superior Maritime Visitor Center, Canal Park, Duluth; 218-727-2497; www.lsmma.com. Get an up-close and personal view of the giant lake carriers as they glide beneath the world famous Aerial Lift Bridge. Walk out to the lighthouse, feed the gulls, then head indoors for one spectacular maritime museum. Videos, model ships and exhibits that feature the Duluth-Superior Harbor and the Great Lakes. Also an on-screen, up-to-the-minute ship schedule. Open daily, year-round. Free admission. NOTE: You can also keep track of the comings and goings of the giant ships by calling the Boat Watchers Hotline, open 24 hours/day in season; 218-722-6489.

Carnival Thrillz, 329 Lake Ave S, Duluth; 218-720-5868; www.carnivalthrillz.com. Carnival Thrillz has rides and games, a huge arcade, Laser Tag, virtual parachute jumping, a NASCAR simulator, a Bungee Trampoline, concessions and waaaaaaaaaay more. Just try to get the kids out of here. Open daily, year-round. Fee charged for the rides and attractions.

DINING

Pizza Lucé, 11 E Superior Street, Duluth; 218-727-7400; www.pizzaluce.com. Extensive menu of traditional and gourmet pizzas, hoagies, salads, hot pastas and desserts. Open daily, year-round (Sun brunch). The Greenery, 200 W 1st Street (in the Holiday Center), Duluth; 218-727-3387. Homemade soups, salads, sandwiches and Bridgeman's ice cream. Open daily, year-round. Vista Fleet, 323 Harbor Dr (waterfront side of the DECC), Duluth; 218-722-6218; www.vistafleet.com. Everyone loves Vista Fleet's Pizza Cruise. It's an hour and a half of cruising and grazing on 4 kinds of pizza and includes an ice cream buffet. They have every kind of topping imaginable so you can build your own sundaes. The pizza and sundae cruise boards at 4:45pm and returns at 6:30pm from the end of June–September on Sundays only. Free for children under age 5. NOTE: The Vista Fleet offers many other cruise and sightseeing tours as well. A narrated history tour of the harbor departs daily, mid-May–mid-Oct. Admission is free for kids under age 5.

LODGING

Comfort Inn-West, 3900 Superior Street W, Duluth; 800-424-6423 or 218-628-1464; www.stayinduluth.com. Indoor pool, spa, free deluxe continental breakfast including Belgian waffles. Comfort Suites Canal Park, 408 Canal Park Dr Duluth; 800-424-6423 or 218-727-1378; www.choicehotels.com/hotel/mn031. Indoor pool, spa and free deluxe continental breakfast. Located on the shores of Lake Superior in Canal Park. Duluth Hampton Inn, 310 Canal Park Dr, Duluth; 800-426-7866 or 218-720-3000; www.duluth.com/hampton. Indoor pool, spa and free continental breakfast. On the shores of Lake Superior in Canal Park. Holiday Inn Hotel & Suites, 200 W 1st Street, Duluth; 800-477-7089 or 218-722-1202; www.hiduluth.com. 2 indoor pools, spa, kids' wading pool, themed KidSuites and 4 on-site restaurants. Free continental breakfast. Spirit Mountain Recreation Area, Mountain Villas, 9525 Skyline Pkwy W, Duluth; 866-688-4552 or 218-624-1949; www.mtvillas.com. Lodging located within a winter downhill ski resort and summer fun park. The 900-square-foot villas feature 2 bedrooms, 2 baths, full kitchens, living rooms and fireplaces. Sleeps six. Open year-round. Spirit Mountain Travel Lodge, 9315 Westgate Blvd, Duluth; 800-777-8530 or 218-628-3691; www.duluth.com/travelodge. Indoor pool, spa, game room and free deluxe continental breakfast. Willard Munger Inn, 7408 Grand Ave (on the trail across from Lake Superior Zoo), Duluth; 800-982-2453 or 218-624-4814; www.mungerinn.com. Located on the Willard Munger and Western Waterfront Trails, the inn offers complimentary use of bikes, canoes, kayaks and paddleboats. Free continental breakfast. Pets welcome. Adjacent campground.

CAMPING

Jay Cooke State Park, 780 Hwy 210, Carlton; 218-384-4610. 82 campsites, 21 electrical; 50 miles of hiking trails, 12 miles of snowmobile trails and 32 miles cross-country ski trails. Trout fishing and whitewater rafting. Duluth Tent & Trailer Camp, 8411 Congdon Blvd (8 miles NE of Duluth on Scenic Hwy 61), Duluth; 218-525-1350. 42 electrical hookups, 12 tent sites and playground. Fond Du Lac Campground, Junction Hwys 23 & 210, Duluth; 218-749-5388 or 218-780-2319. Located on the St. Louis River. Boat launch, docks, fishing pier. Playground in adjoining city park. Open May–Oct. KOA Kampground, 1381 Carlton Rd, Cloquet; 218-879-5726. Campsites and Kamping Kabins. Pool, playground, camp store and gift shop. Open May–mid-Oct. Spirit Mountain, 9500 Spirit Mountain; 800-642-6377, Ext 544 or 218-624-8544; www.spiritmt.com. 73 campsites with electricity, tent sites have fire rings.

Duluth Convention & Visitors Bureau, 21 W Superior Street, Ste 110, Duluth; 800-4-Duluth or 218-722-4011; www.visitduluth.com. Duluth Area Chamber of Commerce, 5 W 1st Street, Duluth; 218-722-5501; www.duluthchamber.com. Duluth Parks and Recreation, 12 E 4th Street, Duluth; 218-723-3337. For trail conditions, call 218-723-3678. Duluth OMNI-MAX Theatre, 310 Harbor Dr, Duluth; 218-727-0022; www.duluthomnimax.com. Open daily, year-round. Port Town Trolley, Duluth. The trolley runs daily Memorial Day–Labor Day. Catch it at Canal Park—the fare is 25 cents. Wheelchair accessible. River's Bend Carriage Service, 4447 Caribou Lake Rd, 218-729-5873. Horse-drawn carriage rides begin at Canal Park, May–Oct. Bicycle Rental & Shuttle Service, Munger Trail Bike Rental, 7408 Grand Ave, Duluth; 800-982-BIKE or 218-624-4814; www.mungerinn.com. Bike rentals and shuttle pickup from most Duluth area motels. Canoe and kayak rentals available. Wheel Fun Rentals, Canal Park (next to Comfort Suites), Duluth; 218-260-7140; www.wheelfunrentals.com. Open daily Memorial Day–Labor Day; weekends only after Labor Day. Seaplane Rides, Orville Air, located at the end of Park Point at Sky Harbor Airport; 218-733-0078. 15–20 minute rides, 2-person minimum. Positive Energy for Youth, located 15 miles north of Duluth near Island Lake, 218-391-0147; www.energy-youth.com. Instructional dog sled and sleigh/hay rides. North Shore Scenic Railroad, The Depot, 506 W Michigan Street, Duluth; 800-423-1273 or 218-722-1273; www.lsrm.org. Narrated train tours along the Lake Superior shoreline and into the Northwoods. Several theme rides to choose from, including a "Pizza Train." May–Oct. (The Depot also houses the Lake Superior Railroad Museum—the home of one of the world's largest steam locomotives. Open daily, year-round.) Lake Superior & Mississippi Railroad, Grand Ave & Fremont Street (across from the zoo), Duluth; 218-624-7549; www.lsmrr.org. 90-minute historic tours along the St. Louis River aboard vintage trains. Weekends mid-June–Sept.

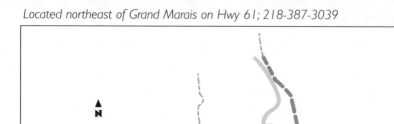

Located northeast of Grand Marais on Hwy 61; 218-387-3039

JUDGE C. R. MAGNEY STATE PARK

POINTS OF INTEREST:
Devil's Kettle, waterfalls, cascades

TOTAL TRAIL MILES: 9
THIS HIKE: 2.5 miles (round-trip)
DIFFICULTY: Moderate
ELEVATION: 200 feet

The Devil's Kettle is the main attraction in the 4,600-acre Judge C. R. Magney State Park. This has to be one of the coolest waterfalls on earth. The Brule River splits around a huge boulder, sending one side of the river careening over a 50-foot drop; the other side falls into a large pothole and no one knows for sure where the water ends up. Dyes and paraphernalia have been dropped into the pothole in an attempt to find the river's exit, but to no avail. So far, the Devil's Kettle is nature's well-kept secret.

Judge C. R. Magney has 9 miles of trails with an elevation gain of 200 feet. The Devil's Kettle hike, part of the Superior Hiking Trail, continues north to Cty 69

68 JUDGE C. R. MAGNEY STATE PARK

WHERE TO BEGIN

From Grand Marais, drive 14 miles northeast on Hwy 61. The park entrance is on the left. Pick up a map at the ranger station. The trailhead begins at the parking lot. It's also the location of an outdoor restroom and drinking water. Cross the footbridge to the north side of the river where you'll find a picnic table and another outdoor restroom. Follow the 1.25-mile trail to the Lower Falls, Upper Falls and Devil's Kettle.

The trails are moderate in difficulty and will prove challenging for young children, but kids ages 6 and older will have a blast exploring like the voyageurs from long ago.

THE TRAILS

Devil's Kettle Trail The 2.5-mile hike to the Devil's Kettle is incredibly scenic, albeit rough. Gravel and sand paths follow the flow of the river, cutting through woods and rising to rocky ledges—no guardrails. About three quarters of a mile into the hike, a root-covered side trail veers left to the 15-foot-high Lower Falls. Back on the main trail another half mile upstream, the trail leads to a long staircase. The steep steps down to the Upper Falls area seem unending, but the view is definitely worth the effort. Continuing on the main drag another 700 feet, you'll find the very quirky Devil's Kettle.

SCAVENGER HUNT (Devil's Kettle Trail)

1. "X" on rock (along footpath)

2. Waterfall

3. Foam

4. Woodpecker holes in tree

5. Tree in path

6. Devil's Kettle sign

TRIVIA QUESTIONS

Q. Why do woodpeckers make holes in trees?

Woodpeckers make holes in trees, especially dead ones, because they are looking for insects to eat. The holes woodpeckers make become homes for other animals like squirrels and kestrels.

Q. Notice all the foam in the river. Does the foam mean the river is polluted?

The foam found on the surface of the Brule River does not mean it is polluted. Decaying plants in the swamps and bogs create an acid that colors the water brown. When the water rushes over the many cascades and falls it becomes aerated (gases and oxygen mix with the water). The acid mixed in with the aerated water causes the foam.

Q. The park is named in honor of Judge C. R. Magney. Why?

Judge Clarence Magney believed everyone, not just rich people, should have the right to enjoy nature in its awesome raw beauty. He helped establish 11 state parks and waysides along Lake Superior for everyone's pleasure.

Q: What is the highest point in Minnesota?

At a whopping 2,301 feet, nearby Eagle Mountain is the highest point in the state. It is a rugged, difficult, 3-mile rocky climb to the top, but the reward is a panoramic view of surrounding lakes and forested hillsides. Most of the trail is in the Boundary Waters Canoe Area Wilderness. Access the trailhead from Forest Service Road #170.

Q: What is the Gunflint Trail?

Originally blazed by Native Americans, the 60-mile trail also became a popular one for the early voyageurs, fur trappers and miners. It begins in Grand Marais and is the entry point for the Boundary Waters Canoe Area Wilderness.

THINGS TO DO IN THE AREA

Grand Marais Rec Park, Hwy 61 & 8th Ave W, Grand Marais; 800-998-0959 or 218-387-1275. Take the kids swimming at the Grand Marais Rec Park. Open to the public, the indoor pool has a diving board, sauna, hot tub and wading pool. Admission charge is minimal.

Hedstrom Lumber Company, 1504 Gunflint Trail (from Hwy 61, turn left onto the Gunflint Trail in Grand Marais; drive north 5 miles to Maple Hill, watch for signs), Grand Marais; 218-387-2995 X 10; www.hedstromlumber.com. Tour the working sawmill and see how trees become boards. mid-June–Labor Day. Call for reservations. Free admission.

North House Folk School, PO Box 759, Grand Marais; 888-387-9762 or 218-387-9762; www.northhouse.org. North House presents hundreds of programs year-round, based on their mission to promote and preserve knowledge, skills and crafts of the past and present. Courses include boat building, tool making, wild rice harvesting, photography, jewelry making and everything in between. In keeping with their hands-on philosophy, they offer 2-hour sailing excursions aboard the schooner *Hjordis*. This course is an introductory to sailing. You'll tour the Grand Marais harbor and Big Lake with its amazing views of the Sawtooth Mountains and North Shore. Board at the school's dock in Grand Marais mid-Jun–Oct at 9. Fee charged.

DINING

Sven & Ole's, Grand Marais; 218-387-1713. Pizza, subs, salads, pasta, sandwiches. Sydney's Frozen Custard, Grand Marais; 218-387-2093. Frozen custard, Chicago-style hot dogs, sandwiches. Victoria's Bake House & Fine Dining, Grand Marais; 218-387-1747. Deli and lunch menu, as well as dinner.

LODGING

Best Western Superior Inn & Suites, Hwy 61 E, Grand Marais; 800-842-8439 or 218-387-2240; www.bestwestern.com/superiorinn. On the shore of Lake Superior. Free deluxe continental breakfast. Harbor Inn Restaurant & Motel, PO Box 669, Grand Marais; 800-595-4566 or 218-387-1191; www.bytheharbor.com. Overlooks the harbor. Free continental breakfast, on-site restaurant with a kids' menu. Naniboujou Lodge, 20 Naniboujou Trail, Grand Marais; 218-387-2688; www.naniboujou.com. On the shore of Lake Superior and directly across the highway from Judge C. R. Magney State Park. Hiking, fishing, agate hunting. On-site restaurant. NOTE: Going hiking? Let the folks at Naniboujou prepare a bag lunch so you can picnic next to one of the many waterfalls found on the trails.

CAMPING

Judge C. R. Magney State Park, 4051 E Hwy 61, Grand Marais; 218-387-3039. 27 campsites (no electric), 1 carry-in site, hiking, fishing, picnic areas. Golden Eagle Lodge & Campground, 468 Clearwater Rd, Grand Marais; 800-346-2203 or 218-388-2203; www.golden-eagle.com. 10 cabins, 9 campsites with electricity, swimming, hiking, biking, canoeing. Free fishing seminars, nature center with a Tepee, campfires and activities. Pontoon, kayak, canoe and boat rentals. On the Gunflint Trail. Open spring to Nov. Grand Marais RV Park and Campground, Hwy 61 & 8th Ave W, Grand Marais; 800-998-0959 or 218-387-1712; www.grandmaraisrvparkandcampground.com. 300 campsites with electric and tent sites. Indoor pools and spa, boat ramps and marina, Lake Superior shoreline. Open May–Oct. Gunflint Pines Resort & Campground, 217 Gunflint Lake S, Grand Marais; 800-533-5814 or 218-388-4454; www.gunflintpines.com. 20 campsites with hookups, tent and cabins. Bathhouse, playground, marina, camp store, fishing, hiking, canoeing, massage and spa. Lodge with limited meals (burgers, pizza, soups, ice cream). Snowmobiles, cross-country skis and boats for rent. **Hungry Jack Lodge & Campground**, 372 Hungry Jack Rd, Grand Marais; 800-338-1566 or 218-388-2265; www.hungryjacklodge.com. RV and tent campground, cabins. Sand beach, playground and sandbox, horseshoes, fishing, hiking, bar and on-site restaurant serve family style. Bike, boat, pontoon and canoe rentals. Fishing guide service, hunting and dock service. Open year-round.

MORE STUFF

Grand Marais Area Chamber of Commerce, PO Box 805, Grand Marais 55604; 218-387-9112; www.grandmarais-mn.com. **Grand Marais Area Tourism Association**, 13 N Broadway, Grand Marais; 218-387-2524; www.grandmarais.com. **Gunflint Trail Association**, 218 Hwy 61, Grand Marais; 218-387-3191; www.gunflint-trail.com. **Boundary Waters Canoe Area Wilderness (BWCAW)** Reservations: 800-745-3399. **Superior National Forest & BWCAW** Information: 218-626-4300; www.fs.fed.us/r9/forests/superior. **Superior Coastal Sports**, PO Box 215, Grand Marais; 800-720-2809 or 218-387-2360; www.superiorcoastal.com. Sea kayak and Windrider Trimaran rentals. Must have experience to rent. Instructions and guided adventure packages. Café inside. Open year-round. **Superior North Outdoor Center**, 9 N Broadway, Grand Marais; 218-387-2186; www.superiornorthoutdoor.com. Bike rentals and repairs, guided tours. **Wilderness Waters Outfitters**, 800-325-5842 or 218-387-2525; www.wilderness-waters.com. Canoeing and camping gear. **Devils Track Nordic Ski Shop**, 218-387-3373; www.devilstracknordic.com. Ski sales, repairs and rentals. **Lake Superior Fishing Charters & Shore Cruises**, 2011 W Hwy 61, Grand Marais; 800-795-8068 or 218-387-1162; www.bear-track.com. Also **Bear Track Outfitting** has canoe, sea kayak, float tube rentals. **Secret Lures Charters**, c/o Grand Marais Rec Area, PO Box 820, Grand Marais; 218-370-1010 (Jun–Sept) or 952-435-7702 (Oct–May). Trout and salmon fishing. **Gunflint Express**, 37 Loon Lake Rd, Grand Marais; 218-388-0616 or 218-370-0857; www.gunflint-trail.com/gex.html. Shuttle service to and from the Gunflint Trail.

Foam

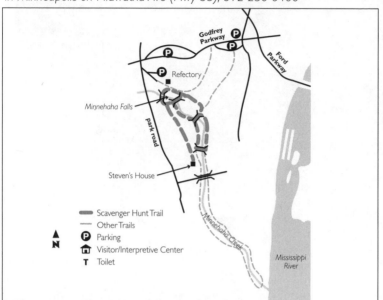

MINNEHAHA FALLS PARK

POINTS OF INTEREST:
Waterfall, Minnehaha Depot, Stevens House,
Longfellow House & Garden

TOTAL TRAIL MILES: 6
THIS HIKE: 2 miles
DIFFICULTY: Easy
ELEVATION: 130 feet

Native Americans have always considered the scenic Minnehaha sacred ground. They called the convergence of the Minnesota and Mississippi Rivers "Mdo-te" and believe it to be the place where creation occurred. Thankfully, much of the area looks the same as it did at the beginning of the twentieth century, so it's easy to understand Longfellow's inspiration for penning his famous poem *Song of Hiawatha*.

Minnehaha was the first wagon trail on the frontier territory and would have been the first state park in the country had Minnesota been able to swing the funds in 1867. Instead, the city of Minneapolis bought the 193 acres of land in 1889 for $100,000. The park attracts more than a half-million visitors annually.

Minnehaha Falls Park has 6 miles of hiking trails with an elevation gain of 130 feet. It also has 12.6 miles of paved bike trails, the famous Longfellow House, the Minnehaha Depot and the John Harrington Stevens House.

WHERE TO BEGIN

Minnehaha Falls Park is at 4801 Minnehaha Ave S, Minneapolis. To get to the park from I-94, take the Cedar Ave exit and drive south, away from downtown. Turn left onto Hiawatha Ave and follow it south. The park entrance is on the left.

The trailhead begins in the picnic area and leads across the bridge to the refectory, where you'll find bike rentals, restrooms, drinking water and a restaurant. Steps descend to the falls. The nearby band shell hosts concerts and events throughout the summer. For a concert schedule, call 612-661-4875.

THE TRAILS

Minnehaha Creek Trail The main trail is a picturesque 3-mile loop along Minnehaha Creek. It follows the creek through woods and marshes all the way to the Mississippi River. Five stone bridges cross the creek at varying intervals, allowing you to decide how far you want to hike. Descend the steps to the second bridge for a spectacular view of the 53-foot-high falls as it tumbles over a limestone ledge. The trail itself is beautiful, falls or no falls. Lush vegetation clings to impressive layered limestone bluffs. At the master marker (found at the fourth bridge), the trail turns into a boardwalk through a marsh. At the end of the boardwalk, a narrow dirt path continues down to the Mississippi and empties onto a sandbar. For those with young children, the path to the river is rather rustic and gets slippery in spots. The trail is open to snowshoeing in the winter.

SCAVENGER HUNT (Minnehaha Creek Trail)

1. Bench on trail

2. Stone footbridge

3. Minnehaha Falls

4. Double surrey

5. Master Map (rock marker)

6. Mask of Chief Little Crow, a Native American leader during the Dakota Conflict

7. Minnehaha Depot (AKA "The Princess Depot")

8. John Harrington Stevens House

TRIVIA QUESTIONS

Q: How high is Minnehaha Falls?

The falls is 53 feet high.

Q: "Minnehaha" is an Ojibwa Indian word. What does it mean?

*"Minnehaha" is actually two words: "mi-ni" means "water" and "ha-ha" means "waterfall."
Loosely translated, "Minnehaha" became known as the "laughing waters."*

Q: Minnehaha wasn't always a park. What was it before it was a park?

*Minnehaha was a busy train stop. As many as 39 train trips a day originated from the
Minnehaha Depot, dubbed "The Princess" because of its ornate gingerbread-like trim.*

Q: Why is the John Harrington Stevens House considered to be the birthplace of Minneapolis?

*The Stevens house was the first home built in Minneapolis. In 1852, the official plans for
both Minneapolis and Hennepin County governments were organized and established in
this house. The house was originally located near St. Anthony Falls.*

Q: Henry Wadsworth Longfellow's 1853 poem *Song of Hiawatha*, about an
Ojibwa warrior, made Minnehaha Falls famous. However, Longfellow
never lived in the area or saw the falls, so how did he know about them?

*Longfellow's inspiration for the poem came from a friend who mailed him pictures of the
falls and provided a detailed description of the area.*

THINGS TO DO IN THE AREA

John Harrington Stevens House, located in Minnehaha Falls Park; 612-722-
2220. The 1850 Stevens House was the first home built in Minneapolis. It was
the social and political hub of the time and considered the birthplace of the
city, as well as Hennepin County. Stevens ran a ferry at St. Anthony Falls—the
only falls on the Mississippi River. It is open for tours May–Sept on Sat & Sun;
Small admission fee charged.

Minnehaha Depot, located in the park. Built in the 1870s, the depot is known
as "The Princess" because of its delicate Victorian era gingerbread-like trim.

During its peak, nearly 40 trains a day passed through this little station. It closed in 1963 and was turned over to the city. Guided tours of the depot are on Sundays throughout the summer. This is a great chance to learn how the station communicated using Morse code. Free admission.

Longfellow House Hospitality Center & Garden, 4800 Minnehaha Ave (at the northwest end of the park); 612-230-6520. Contrary to what the name suggests, the Longfellow House was neither built nor lived in by the famous poet. Constructed in 1906 by a New York businessman, the two-story house is a $^2/_3$-scale replica of Longfellow's, who lived in Cambridge, Massachusetts, at the time. The Longfellow House is free and open year-round, Mon–Fri. The garden is adjacent. Some original elements are still present such as the gorgeous carved fireplace, but the house primarily functions as a history center and to provide information for the **Grand Rounds National Scenic Byway**, a 50-mile outdoor recreational loop. The Grand Rounds is totally encompassed by a major urban area, with seven interpretive districts:

- **Downtown Riverfront:** 1.2 miles of highlights that include St. Anthony Falls (the only true waterfall on the entire Mississippi River), paddleboat and trolley rides, the Old Milling District and the famous Stone Arch Bridge—the only stone bridge that crosses the Mississippi.
- **Mississippi River:** 9.2 miles of river exploration and the opportunity to hike an ancient Native American path.
- **Minnehaha:** 12.6 miles of trails, half of which follow the picturesque Minnehaha Creek.
- **Chain of Lakes:** 13.3 miles of lakeside paths, canoeing from Lake Calhoun to Brownie Lake, the Como-Harriet Streetcar line (still operating), outdoor concerts at the Lake Harriet Bandshell and a bird sanctuary, rose gardens and Peace Gardens, all located near Lake Harriet.
- **Theodore Wirth:** 4 miles within Minneapolis' largest park. Highlights: Eloise Butler Garden and Sanctuary (the oldest wildflower garden in the nation), a sand beach with lifeguards, a quaking bog.
- **Victory Memorial:** 3.8 miles commemorating Hennepin County's WWI veterans.
- **Northeast:** 6 miles of downtown skyline view. See where barges, trains and trucks deliver their goods.

Historic Fort Snelling, at Hwys 5 & 55 (1 mile east of the International Airport), St. Paul; 612-726-1171; www.mnhs.org/fortsnelling. Established in 1819 as a military outpost, Fort Snelling is now a living history museum. Costumed guides offer a taste of fort life as it was in the 1800s. Talk with soldiers, trade fur skins with a Dakota Indian, help with the laundry using a washboard and watch the blacksmith at his forge. Learn how to shoulder a musket, mend clothes and scrape a hide. Partake in the daily cannon shoot. The History Center has films and changing exhibits. Walk or bike the dozens of trails. One leads to Minnehaha Falls Park (1.2 miles). Fort Snelling is open daily Memorial Day–Labor Day; May, Sept & Oct, Sat–Sun. Admission charged; free for children ages 5 and under. The History Center is open year-round.

Mall of America, 60 E Broadway (at the junction of I-494 & Hwy 77), Bloomington; 800-490-4200 or 952-883-8800; www.mallofamerica.com. The gigantic Mall of America is the largest of its kind in the United States. Almost 50 million people from all over the world visit annually. There are more than 500 stores, 50 restaurants, 8 nightclubs, a 14-screen mega-movie theater, bowling alley and a walk-through aquarium featuring sharks and hundreds of other sea creatures. But let's get to the point: the major kid attraction is an indoor amusement park that features over two dozen rides, including a full-scale roller coaster and an 18-hole miniature golf course. The LEGO Imagination Center has changing exhibits and hands-on activities. Open daily, year-round. Free parking and admission, but there is a charge for rides and attractions.

DINING

Sea Salt Eatery, 4801 Minnehaha Ave S (in the park next to the bike rental); 612-721-8990. Squid tacos and fried oysters are just a small sampling of the seafood served. Everything on the menu is ocean related, with the exception of Minnesota's own Summit beer and Sebastian Joe's ice cream. Casual indoor dining or enjoy the outdoor terrace for some great people watching.

LODGING

Comfort Inn-Airport, 1321 E 78th Street; (I-494 at Portland/12th Ave exit), Bloomington; 952-854-3400; www.hotelchoice.com/hotel/MN015. Free continental breakfast, complimentary Mall of America and airport shuttle service, restaurant and lounge, indoor pool. Days Inn Bloomington, 7851 Normandale Blvd (off I-94/Hwy 100), Bloomington; 800-329-7466 or 952-835-7400; www.daysinnbloomington.com. Free continental breakfast, 24-hour pool, free transportation to the Mall of America and airport. The Residence Inn at the Depot, 225 3rd Ave S, Minneapolis; 800-331-3131 or 612-375-1700; www.thedepotminneapolis.com. Offers just about every kind of lodging, including luxury suites with full kitchens. They also have a downtown shuttle service, complimentary breakfast, restaurant, bar and giant indoor water park. The water park is over 15,000 square feet with 4 pools, a 185-foot-high waterslide, splash fountain, game room, giant screen TV, glass atrium and snack bar serving pizza, hot dogs and ice cream. Open Thurs–Sun. Passes are available for non-hotel guests on a limited basis for about $15. The Depot is within walking distance of the Mississippi River, Hubert H. Humphrey Dome, Historic Mill District, Target Center and theatre district. The Depot Rink is next door to the hotel. The indoor seasonal figure skating rink (5th Ave & Washington;

612-339-2253) is underneath a restored 600-foot-long wrought iron train shed. Floor-to-ceiling windows fill the rink with natural light and present gorgeous city views. It is open to the public and offers concessions, coin lockers, heated underground parking, skate rental and sharpening. Admission charged.

CAMPING

Lebanon Hills Regional Park Campground, 12100 Johnny Cake Ridge Rd, Apple Valley; 952-454-9211; www.co.dakota.mn.us/parks/index.htm. 82 sites with electricity, 11 tent sites. Nice beach, horse rentals and hiking. Close to the Minnesota Zoo. Lowry Grove Campground, 2501 Lowry Ave NE, St. Anthony; 612-781-3148. Full hookups only, no tenting and no dogs. St. Paul East KOA, 568 Cottage Grove Dr, Woodbury; 800-562-3640 or 651-436-6436; www.stpaulkoa.com. 76 sites including tent sites; cabins, heated pool, playground and recreation room. Open mid-Apr–mid-Oct.

MORE STUFF

Greater Minneapolis Convention & Visitors Association, 250 Marquette Ave S, Minneapolis 55401; 888-445-MPLS or 612-767-8000; www.minneapolis.org. Also check out the Minneapolis website designed specifically for a getaway with the kids: www.minneapolis-kids.org. Minneapolis Metro North CVB, 6200 Shingle Creek Pkwy, #248, Minneapolis 55430; 800-541-4364 or 763-566-7722; www.justaskmn.com. Minneapolis Parks and Recreation Board, 2117 West River Rd N, Minneapolis; 612-230-6400; www.minneapolisparks.org. See these folks for parking permits and information about the Grand Rounds National Scenic Byways system. St. Paul Convention & Visitors Bureau, 175 W Kellogg Blvd, #502; St. Paul 55102; 800-627-6101 or 651-265-4900; www.visitstpaul.com. Wheel Fun Rental, located in Minnehaha Falls Park; 320-247-2162. Open daily, Memorial Day–Labor Day (fall season is weekends only). A wide variety of bike rentals from double surreys to quad sports to kids' bikes. AMC Theatres, 401 South Ave (in the Mall of America), Bloomington; 952-851-0074; www.mallofamerica.com. 14 theaters! Check out shows and times on the web. Crown Theatres, Block E, 600 Hennepin Ave S, Minneapolis; 612-338-5900. 15-theater complex. RiverCity Trolley, 612-204-0000 or 612-378-7833; www.rivercitytrolley.org. Ride the trolley May–Oct. Anson Northrup Paddleboat, Boom Island, Plymouth Ave & NE 8th Street, Minneapolis; 612-661-4800. Side-wheeler with two deck levels and restrooms on board. $1 fee for parking on island. Light Rail Transit, 800-NEW-RIDER or 612-373-3333; www.metrotransit.org/rail. 17 stations connect the airport, Mall of America and downtown Minneapolis. Children ages 5 and under are free with paid adult. Trains run daily. Purchase tickets at vending machines located on station platforms.

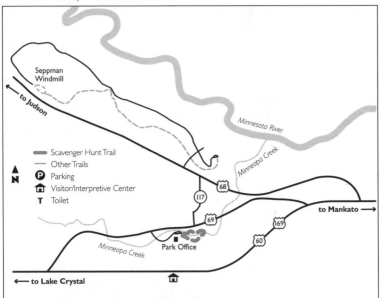

MINNEOPA STATE PARK

POINTS OF INTEREST:
Double waterfall, sandstone cliffs,
Seppman Windmill, natural prairie

TOTAL TRAIL MILES: 4.5
THIS HIKE: 0.75 mile (round-trip)
DIFFICULTY: Easy
ELEVATION: 45 feet

The 1,145-acre Minneopa State Park is divided into two parks: the waterfall section and the prairie and camping area, which is a couple miles north of the main park entrance.

Since the 1800s, the area around the Minneopa Creek has been a public favorite for several reasons: the double waterfalls, gorgeous sandstone river gorge and hardwood forest, glacial till (leftover earthen debris from 14,000 years ago), the tallgrass prairie and the nostalgic history of the Seppman Windmill.

The park has 4.5 miles of trails with an elevation gain of 45 feet. The extremely popular half-mile waterfall hike offers many awesome views of two waterfalls. It is also paved up to the stairs, making for a nice stroll beneath a canopy of maples. The 1-mile Seppman Windmill hike is much more secluded. The grassy path winds through a woods, over a small creek and up a flight of stairs to the mill. The kids will love this park!

WHERE TO BEGIN

From Mankato, the easiest way to find the main entrance is to travel west on Hwy 169 and watch for signs as you approach the Hwy 68 junction.

The 4.5 miles of trails are fairly easy, but the path to the bottom of the falls does involve some steps and can get slippery in spots. The prairie trails are grassy paths posing little danger for young children. The park at the falls has a huge picnic shelter, nature center with hands-on displays, restrooms, drinking water, benches along the river, a footbridge and a paved path to the stairs that lead to the bottom of the falls. There is another restroom at Seppman Windmill.

THE TRAILS

Falls Trail A crowd pleaser, the 0.75-mile falls hike gives an up-close and personal view of two roaring waterfalls. The first falls drops approximately 15 feet and the second falls has a drop of about 30 feet. The paved interpretive trail crosses the Minneopa River near the parking lot and explains the natural erosion process that created the falls. Beyond the trail is a stairway that curves around a spectacular sandstone wall. Continue on the footbridge over the creek and follow the narrow path through the sandstone canyon to the base of the falls. Watch the birds fly in and out of their summer homes in the cliffs. NOTE: Swimming and wading are forbidden.

Seppman Windmill Trail Once a sheep pasture, there are several trails through the restored prairie leading to the Seppman Windmill. The shortest is a wide, 1-mile (one-way) grassy hike through the woods and up a flight of stairs to the mill and a panoramic view of the whole river valley, treetop to treetop. The trailhead begins at a dirt parking spot found about midway along the main gravel road. The road features interpretive signs and proceeds straight to the mill, where you'll find a portable restroom and a bench at the overlook.

The refurbished 1864 mill no longer has its wind vanes and the granary was completely rebuilt in 1970 on top of the original foundation. The granary was used as storage for the grain as it came in to be milled into flour. Speculation has it some of the customers used the granary as a place to get a little shut-eye until their grain was milled.

SCAVENGER HUNT (Falls Trail)

1. Double waterfall

2. Sandstone cliff

3. Wood footbridge

4. "Bird" shape in sandstone cliff

5. "Africa" shape in sandstone cliff

6. Bird homes in cliff

7. Parmeloid lichen cliff

TRIVIA QUESTIONS

Q: "Minneopa" is a Dakota Indian word. What does it mean?

The word "Minneopa" means "water falling twice."

Q: The tallgrass prairie of North America was once the largest continuous ecosystem on the continent. Before the pioneers, Minnesota boasted 18 million acres of prairie. How much of it remains today?

Less than one-tenth of 1 percent of the tallgrass prairie is in existence today. Minneopa State Park is a very small piece of the remaining tallgrass prairie.

Q: What prairie grasses are native to the park?

The native park grasses include Kentucky bluegrass, smooth brome, little bluestem, big bluestem, Indian grass and side-oats grama.

Q: About once every three or four years, park managers light a fire in the prairie called a "controlled burn." Why do they do that?

Controlled fires can be good for the prairie because they reduce weeds and get rid of other non-native plants that choke out all the native plants.

Q: There are deep rock walls along the Minneopa falls. The rock is very soft and easy to scratch. What kind of rock is it?

The soft rock walls found in the park are sandstone. The eroding force of Minneopa Creek on the sandstone continues moving the falls away from where they began at the Minnesota River.

THINGS TO DO IN THE AREA

Bike/hike. The City of Mankato has more than 50 miles of paved bike/hike trails that follow streams, the river and wetlands and give a historical view of city landmarks such as the foundry and quarries. Pick up a free trail map at the Mankato Chamber of Commerce, 112 Riverfront Dr. The Chamber is an unmanned location in a vintage railcar next to the old depot.

Mount Kato, 20461 Hwy 66, Mankato; 800-668-5286 or 507-625-3363; www.mountkato.com. Probably more well known as a winter ski resort, Mount Kato has over 7 miles of mountain bike trails that cut through woods, skirt ponds and travel over ski trails. The trails are open May–October. Fee charged. Bike rental available.

Sakatah Singing Hills State Trail, Trail Office; 507-267-4772; www.trailsfrom-rails.com/sakatah_singing_trail. "Sakatah" is the Dakota Indian word for "singing hills." The level, 39-mile paved trail stretches from Mankato to Faribault, winding through a dozen lakes, a forested state park and three friendly small towns. Restrooms and drinking water are found at mile 16 in Elysian, at mile 25 at Sakatah State Park and at mile 35 at Shager County Park on Cannon Lake; portable restrooms only at the Mankato trailhead, located a quarter mile north of the Hwys 14 & 22 interchange on Lime Valley Rd. Swim or camp in Sakatah Lake State Park or take a break and see the sights in one of the small towns. Elysian has a cute coffee and ice cream shop in a little red schoolhouse called A Step Back in Time (410 Hwy 60 west). It is open daily, year-round. 507-267-4055. Elysian is about midpoint on the trail.

Sibley Park, located off S Riverfront Dr; 507-387-8649. Mankato has more than 30 parks—Sibley is the largest and definitely a must-see while in Mankato. For starters, there's a free zoo with over 30 species of animals and birds—a favorite is prairie dog town. These little guys are hilarious to watch as they pop in and out of their holes. There are also tennis courts, ball diamonds, gorgeous flower gardens and a huge winter sliding hill. Open daily.

Tourtellotte Pool, 300 Mabel Street, Mankato; 507-387-7946. You'll get a great workout in the Olympic-sized Tourtellotte Pool. There's also diving, a wading pool, concessions, picnic grounds, a playground, tennis courts and softball diamonds. Open daily June–August. Admission charged.

Hiniker Pond, Frontage Rd on Hwy 169 N, Mankato; 507-387-8649. Hiniker Pond has a large sand beach, bathhouse, picnic shelter, restrooms, hiking trails and fishing. No lifeguard on duty, so swim at your own risk. Open June–August.

Duck Lake Park, located on the southern shore of Duck Lake off Cty 187, a half mile north of the City of Madison Lake; 507-243-3864. This is a nice day-use park with swimming, a bathhouse, playground, volleyball, picnicking, fishing and canoe and paddleboat rentals.

DINING

Big Ed's Chicago Style Hot Dogs, Riverhills Mall, Adams Street (exit at Hwys 14 & 22); 507-388-2016. Bet you can't guess what's on the menu here—hot dogs with all the fixings. Open for lunch and dinner. Chevy's, 119 Front Street (near the riverfront), Mankato; 507-345-1446. Family oriented, Chevy's serves pizzas, burgers and a luncheon salad bar. Open for lunch and dinner. Enchanted Forest, 529 N Riverfront Dr (corner of N Riverfront Dr & Elm Street); 507-385-1448. The Enchanted Forest is a charming gift shop offering books, soaps, candles, gift items, confectionaries and "Old Town" ice cream! Have them scoop up the local favorite (the Minnesota Special) or try a Moose Lake Fudge Cone. They also serve old-fashioned sodas and floats featuring the state's own Spring Grove sodas.

LODGING

AmericInn, 240 Stadium Rd (near the university campus), 800-634-3444 or 507-345-8011; www.americinn.com. Indoor pool and spa, game room and free continental breakfast. Comfort Inn, 131 Apache Place (Hwy 22 S, at Madison Ave), 800-4CHOICE or 507-388-5107; www.choicehotels.com. Heated indoor pool and spa, free continental breakfast, children under 18 stay free with parent. Country Inn & Suites by Carlson, 1900 Premier Dr (junction of Hwys 14 & 22), Mankato; 800-964-7905 or 507-388-8555; www.countryinns.com/mankatomn. Heated indoor pool and spa, T.G.I Friday's restaurant on site. Days Inn, 1285 Range Street (corner of Hwys 169 & 14), 800-DAYS INN or 507-387-3332. Heated indoor pool and spa, game room, free continental breakfast. Fairfield Inn by Marriott, 141 Apache Pl (from Hwy 22 S, drive west on Madison Ave, right on Apache Pl, next to Red Lobster), 800-228-2800 or 507-396-1220; www.marriott.com/mktfi. Heated indoor pool and spa, free continental breakfast with Belgian waffles; kids under 18 stay free with parent. Holiday Inn Downtown, 101 E Main Street (from Hwy 169 take the Riverfront Dr exit), 800-HOLIDAY or 507-345-1234. Indoor pool and spa, sauna, restaurant and lounge on site, exercise room; kids 19 and under stay free with parent.

CAMPING

Minneopa State Park, 54497 Gadwall Rd, Mankato; 507-389-5464. Large campground with hookups and primitive sites; one camper cabin for rent. Double waterfall, historic Seppman Windmill, hiking, biking, fishing, picnic shelter, nature center, horseshoes, volleyball. **Bray County Park**, 22214 Oriole Rd (off Cty 48, 2 miles southeast of the City of Madison Lake), Madison Lake 56063; 507-243-3885. 33 campsites with electricity, 10 tent sites. Paved nature trail, hiking, suspension footbridge, playground, picnic, fishing, canoe and paddleboat rentals. **Kamp Dels**, 14842 Sakatah Lake Rd, Waterville 56096; 507-362-8616; www.kampdels.com. 300 campsites; electric hookups and primitive available. Outdoor heated pool/water park, kiddie pool, petting zoo, mini golf, boats and pontoons,paddleboats, horse and pony rides, tennis court, volleyball, basketball, bikes and fishing. **Kiesler's Campground and RV Resort**, (from Hwy 14, east edge of town), Waseca; 800-533-4642 or 507-835-3179; www.kieslers.com. 300 campsites; electric and primitive. Outdoor heated pool, waterslide and kiddie pool, 18-hole mini golf, playground, recreation hall, camp store, snack bar, boat/motor rental, hiking, basketball, volleyball, horseshoes, planned activities, live entertainment. Open mid-April–September.

MORE STUFF

Mankato Chamber of Commerce, 112 Riverfront Dr; 800-657-4733 or 507-345-4519. Free bike/hike trail map. (Mankato has more than 50 miles of paved trails.) **Greater Mankato Visitors Center**, River Hills Mall (next to Movies 8), 1850 Adams Street, Mankato 56001-4840; 507-388-1100; www.greatermankato.com. **City of North Mankato**, 1001 Belgrade Ave; 507-625-4141. **Mankato MoonDogs Baseball**, Franklin Rogers Field (from Hwy 169 take Downtown exit, turn east into town, left at 4th Street, right on Madison Ave, left on Long Street, left on Caledonia Street, right on Reed Street, park is on the right); 507-625-7047; www.mankatomoondogs.com. **Minnesota Vikings Training Camp**, Minnesota State University, Mankato Campus (from Hwy 169, take the Riverfront Dr exit, go left on Riverfront Dr, then right on Stoltzman Rd, left on Stadium Rd to Monks Ave, park in lots 20-23); 800-657-4733 or 507-345-4519; www.vikingstrainingcamp.com. Annual professional training camp held end of July–mid-August. Daily admission charged to Vikings Village; free for children ages 5 and under. Small parking fee. **Movies 8**, River Hills Mall, Adams Street (exit at Hwys 14 & 22); 507-625-3553; www.riverhillsmall.com. **Canoe and paddleboat rental**. Duck Lake Park, 507-243-3864 and Bray Park, 507-243-3885. **Bike rental**. Mount Kato, Mankato; 507-625-3363 and Lakeside Campground, Elysian; 507-267-4560. **Theatre**. Mankato has an extensive performing arts theatre schedule. Call the Mankato Area Chamber for information or check out their Website; www.mankato.com.

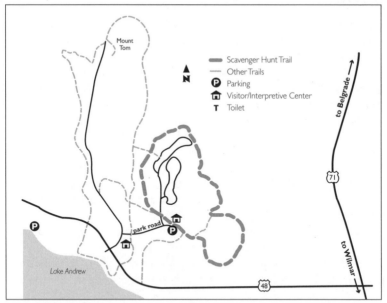

MOUNT TOM, SIBLEY STATE PARK

POINTS OF INTEREST:
Boardwalk through a marsh, Mount Tom
lookout point, nice swimming beach

TOTAL TRAIL MILES: 18
THIS HIKE: 2-mile loop
DIFFICULTY: Easy
ELEVATION: Not a factor

The 2,936-acre state park owes its name to the state's first governor, Henry
Hastings Sibley—an avid hunter who favored the region for its many lakes and
thick woods. The park also boasts the highest vantage for 50 miles around.
Mount Tom, at an elevation of 1,375 feet above sea level, has been visited for
centuries by many people for both strategic and spiritual reasons.

Sibley State Park has 18 miles of trails with an elevation gain of 185 feet from
the lake to Mount Tom. Most trails are easy, either paved or crushed rock, with
lots of interesting focal points geared for everyone.

WHERE TO BEGIN

Sibley State Park is 15 miles north of Willmar on Hwy 71; turn left on Cty 48. Pick up a trail map at the park office, then drive east to the interpretive center. The center features many hands-on displays, slide shows, naturalist-lead programs (seasonal), restrooms and drinking water. Call ahead for hours of operation, as it isn't always open—so plan accordingly. There are three hiking trails and a bike trail that originate from the center's parking lot.

The swimming beach, picnic area, boat launch, fishing pier and ball field are directly west of the park office. The kids will love this place. The beach is clean and has a bathhouse and concessions. The picnic area is up the hill from the beach in a shaded grove and overlooks Lake Andrew. Both areas have restrooms and drinking water.

THE TRAILS

Pondview/Parker Fremberg Trail This easy 2-mile loop is a combination of three ecosystems and two separate trails: Pondview and Parker Fremberg. It is gravel, but fairly level; young children will have no problem navigating it. The trail begins at the interpretive center parking lot, as does the paved bike trail. To find the trailhead, stay to the left on the gravel (the bike path is paved). The hike circles a pond (cuts right through it, actually) via a boardwalk, then heads through a tallgrass prairie and an oak savanna.

Mount Tom Trail This 3.2-mile loop does get a bit rough at times with an elevation climb of about 185 feet. Kids under 6 years old might find it a bit long and challenging. Park in the interpretive center lot, cross the road and follow trail marker 3. Enter the woods and follow the trail to the top of Mount Tom. The trail turns to pavement and leads to the impressive granite and timber lookout tower for a panoramic view of the surrounding lakes and forest. For the return trip, head west of the parking lot to pick up the trail. It leads to Lake Andrew and the beach. For a shortcut that bypasses the beach, cut across the woods on Oak Hills Trail.

NOTE: If you're not in the mood for a hike but don't want to miss the impressive Mount Tom view, you're in luck because there's a road you can drive on to the lookout.

Bike Trail While not a specified hiking trail per se, this is a very scenic, 2-mile (one-way) paved stroll that begins at the interpretive center parking lot. The stroller-friendly trail travels through the woods, across the highway and follows Lake Andrew's shoreline to the beach. Interpretive signs inform about plants and animals in the region. The beach has concessions, a bathhouse with restrooms and canoe rentals. The picnic area is up the hill a short distance from the beach. It also has restrooms, a shelter, drinking water and grills.

SCAVENGER HUNT (Pondview/Parker Fremberg Trail)

1. Mallard duck nesting box with a Canada Goose platform

2. Boardwalk through the marsh

3. White-tailed deer

4. Milkweed

5. Old stone barn foundation

6. Bulb on plant from parasite

7. Woodpecker holes in tree

TRIVIA QUESTIONS

Q: Sibley State Park is located in Kandiyohi County. What does the word "Kandiyohi" mean?

"Kandiyohi" is a Native American word that means "where the buffalo-fish come." It refers to the large numbers of fish found in the local lakes. There are 361 lakes in the county.

Q: Sibley State Park is named in honor of a person. Who is that person?

The park is named after Henry Hastings Sibley, Minnesota's first governor. Governor Sibley hunted in the woods of Kandiyohi.

Q: Name the trees found in the forest of Sibley State Park.

The trees found in the park forest are: oak, red cedar, ironwood, green ash, aspen, maple and basswood.

Q: What is the name of the highest point in Sibley State Park?

The highest point in the park is called Mount Tom. It has an elevation of 1,375 feet above sea level and is one of the highest points for 50 miles. Climb the unusual granite and timber lookout tower for a great view of the surrounding area.

Q: Many white-tailed deer live in the park. When you shine a light on them, why does it appear as if their eyes are glowing?

White-tailed deer are active at night so they need special night vision. They have a reflecting layer behind the retina called a tapetum. The tapeta (plural) helps the deer see better in the dark by giving the light that enters the eyes a second chance to trigger light-sensing cells. The light bounces off the tapeta and back to you, making it look like the deer's eyes are shining. Some other animals with tapeta are skunks, frogs, cats and dogs.

THINGS TO DO IN THE AREA

Flanders River Ranch, 20051 262nd Ave NE (located 2 miles west of Paynesville), Paynesville; 320-243-3453; www.exploreminnesota.com/attractions/7839.html. Flanders River Ranch offers personalized trail rides on horseback along the scenic Crow River. They are open daily May–Sept and by appointment throughout the year.

Timber Frame Ranch, 616 270th Ave NW (20 miles north of Willmar, 2 miles west off Cty 34), New London; 320-354-3518. Take a horse-drawn hay or sleigh ride, depending on the season, pulled by Percherons. Timber Frame Ranch is open year-round with spectacular gardens and orchards for viewing through the growing season and ice skating and cross-country skiing through the winter months. Cozy up to the wood-burning stove in their warming house. Fee charged, children ages 5 and under free with paid adult.

Wetzel's Hayrides and Sleigh Rides, 480 Cty 27 NE, Spicer; 320-796-0056. Wetzel's rides take you over hill and dale through their woods. Open year-round. Fee charged.

Dorothy Olson Aquatic Center, 1601 22nd Street SW, Willmar, 320-214-0114. The aquatic center has two diving boards, two mega-giant waterslides, a kiddie splash area and concessions. You must be at least 48 inches tall to ride the giant waterslides. Open daily throughout the summer. Fee charged.

J & L Bison Ranch, 5650 41st Ave NW, Willmar; 320-235-8465; www.jlbison.com. Take a bus tour to view 300 bison that roam 200 acres of land. J & L Bison Ranch is open mid-Apr–Oct for tours on Tues, Wed and Thurs. Small fee charged.

Little Crow Water Ski Team, Neer Park, 311 2nd Avenue NE, New London; 320-354-5684; www.littlecrow.com. The national award-winning ski team puts on a great show every Friday night throughout the summer months. Watch these fearless folks do their stunts including barefoot jumping, ballet and building human pyramids. On-site concessions. Fee charged; preschool children are free with paid adult.

DINING

Glacial Ridge Ice Cream Shoppe & Pie House, Hwy 23 NE between Spicer and New London; 320-796-5307. This is the place to take the kids. Ron and Kim Wothe turned their apple orchard hobby into a full-time business of creating fun for kids of all ages. They serve soups, sandwiches, every kind of pie (no kidding!) and ice cream. For a very nominal fee, you can take a ride through the apple orchard, or join in on any of the fun activities such as pie making, pumpkin carving, a dress-up-your-pet contest and more. Different activities planned for each weekend. Open daily, May–Dec. Call for winter hours. Jake's Pizza, 316 Litchfield Ave W, Willmar; 320-235-1714. Jake's serves personal pan pizzas along with large pies. Open daily, year-round. LuLu Bean's, 1020 1st Street S, Willmar; 320-214-9633. LuLu Bean's is a coffee house, but serves sandwiches-to-go along with tasty soups. Open daily, year-round. McMillan's Restaurant, 2620 Hwy 71 S, Willmar; 320-235-7213. Full menu, family friendly. Open year-round, 24 hours/day.

LODGING

AmericInn Lodge & Suites of Litchfield, 1525 E Hwy 12; 320-693-1600. Indoor heated pool and spa, free deluxe continental breakfast. Comfort Inn Willmar, 2200 E Hwy 12, Willmar; 800-424-6423 or 320-231-2601. Pool and spa, free continental breakfast. Holiday Inn & Conference Center Willmar, 2100 E Hwy 12, Willmar; 800-465-4983 or 320-235-6060; www.holidayinnwillmar.com. Pool, kiddie pool and spa. On-site restaurant. Northern Inn Hotel & Suites, 154 Lake Ave S, Spicer; 800-941-0423 or 320-796-2091; www.northerninn.com. Indoor pool and spa, breakfast bar, sand beach, fishing. Pontoon boat rental. Adjacent to a restaurant and bar. Scotwood Motel, 1017 E Frontage Rd (E Hwy 12), Litchfield; 800-225-5489 or 320-693-2496; www.scotwoodmotel.com. Indoor heated pool and spa, free breakfast.

CAMPING

Sibley State Park, 800 Sibley Park Rd NE, New London; 320-354-2055. 134 campsites (53 electric), group tent sites, horseback riders group camp. Large picnic area with grills, swimming beach with concessions and bathhouse, restrooms, fishing, boat and canoe rentals, hiking, biking, snowmobiling, cross-country skiing, park store. Island View Resort on Nest Lake, 5910 132nd Ave NE, Spicer; 800-421-9708 or 320-796-2775; www.islandviewresort-nestlake.com. 12 cabins, campfires with free firewood, sand beach, hydro-bikes, playground and rec room. Free boat, canoes, paddleboats and bikes. Rental charge for pontoon and ski boat. Small campground with hookups. Open May–Sept. Lake Ripley Resort & Motel, 126 Marshall Ave N, Litchfield; 320-693-7201. Motel and 35 campsites on the lake. Boat launch, fishing, swimming, playground and park.

MORE STUFF

Willmar Area Visitors Bureau, 2104 E Hwy 12, Willmar 56201; 800-845-8747; www.seeyouinwillmar.com. Spicer Bike & Sports, 178 Progress Way, Spicer; 320-796-6334; www.spicerbike-sports.com. Bike and rollerblade rentals. Sibley State Park, 800 Sibley Park Rd NE, New London; 888-646-6367 or 651-296-6157. Canoe and rowboat rentals. Carmike Cinemas, Kandi Mall, 1605 S 1st Street, Willmar; 320-235-3811. Twin Spin Cinema, 151 Progress Circle, Spicer; 320-796-5500; www.twinspincinema.com. The Barn Theatre, 321 4th Ave SW (downtown), Willmar; 320-235-9500; www.thebarntheatre.com. Live theatre; performances year-round.

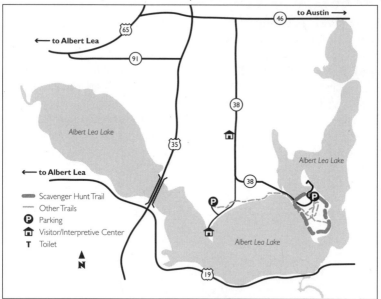

3 miles southeast of Albert Lea on Cty 38; 507-379-3403

to Austin →
to Albert Lea →
to Albert Lea ←
to Albert Lea ←

Albert Lea Lake
Albert Lea Lake
Albert Lea Lake

Scavenger Hunt Trail
Other Trails
Parking
Visitor/Interpretive Center
Toilet

N

MYRE-BIG ISLAND STATE PARK

POINTS OF INTEREST:
White pelicans, Albert Lea Lake, esker

TOTAL TRAIL MILES: 16
THIS HIKE: 2 miles
DIFFICULTY: Easy
ELEVATION: Not a factor

If you want a taste of the "real" Minnesota, head to Myre-Big Island State Park. The 116-acre island, which is actually a peninsula, supports one of the best examples of a hardwood forest. The remaining 1,480 acres is a thriving prairie and marshland much like what greeted the first pioneers when they arrived. Evidence of the Ice Age is everywhere, from the shallow riverbed that is now Albert Lea Lake to the 30-foot-high esker gravel ridge left behind by the melting glacier.

Myre-Big Island State Park has 16 miles of trails with an elevation gain of 30 feet. The quick loop through the center of Big Island is paved and perfect for young children or those in a stroller. There is an interpretive center on Big Lake said to house one of the state's largest prehistoric artifact collections, but it was closed during our visit with no real timeline for reopening. The Esker Trail is also closed from time to time due to wet weather conditions.

WHERE TO BEGIN

Big Island is located 3 miles southeast of Albert Lea, on Cty 38. Signs direct you to the park from Interstates 90 & 35. Getting lost is a near impossibility. Cty 38 leads straight to the island.

The Big Island has two restrooms, drinking water, a nice grassy picnic area and camping with electricity. Primitive camping and canoe rental available on Little Island. For those with young children, Big Island has beautiful paved and dirt trails under a full tree canopy and many opportunities for spotting deer, squirrels, woodpeckers and white pelicans.

THE TRAILS

Big Island Trail The 2-mile Blue Diamond dirt trail hugs the island perimeter with a continuous view of Albert Lea Lake. At its widest, the trail is about 4 feet, narrowing to 18 inches at the very tip of the island. A few strategically placed benches along the way provide a nice lake view. This is an interesting, easy hike kids will like with very little in the line of danger for parents to concern themselves over. There are a few side trails leading to the lake, but the lake itself is very shallow (around 6 feet). This is also your best bet for viewing white pelicans. These large birds have a wingspan close to 6 feet. The inland hike through the hardwood forest is approximately a half mile long and paved.

Great Marsh Trail This is an easy 2.25-mile loop through a marshy wetland. Expect to see white pelicans along the lakeside part of the hike, especially during fall migration. Common plants to be on the lookout for are cattails, water lilies, wild irises and marsh marigolds.

Esker Trail The easy 5-mile (round-trip) hike winds through shoulder-high prairie grass. The wide grassy trail gives the kids a chance to see what prairie life might have looked like to pioneers like Laura Ingalls-Wilder. It's a short steep climb to the top of the esker, which is about 30 feet high and a half mile long. A shaded picnic area and drinking water are found close to the train tracks. Benches on the trail at overlooks of the prairie and lake views.

SCAVENGER HUNT (Big Island Trail)

1. Big Island sign

2. American White Pelican

3. Deer tracks

4. Tree with hollow center

5. Jack-in-the-pulpit (red fruit in the fall)

6. Little Island sign

7. Lily pads

8. Maple leaf

TRIVIA QUESTIONS

Q: What is an esker?

An esker is a winding ridge of sand and gravel left by the glacier as it melted away.

Q: Big Island is an excellent example of a hardwood forest. Name some of the trees found on the island.

Hardwood trees found on Big Island include maple, basswood, ash, elm, ironwood and oak.

Q: Much of Myre-Big Island State Park is prairie, with the exception of the hardwood forest found on Big Island. Why are there are so few trees in the rest of the park?

Years ago, prairie wildfires swept through the region, preventing trees from taking root. Surrounded by water, Big Island was protected from the fires and the trees grew.

Q: Birds of prey are called raptors. How many Big Island raptors can you name?

The Big Island raptors include American Kestrels, Marsh Hawks, Red-tailed Hawks, Rough-legged Hawks, Great Horned Owls and Bald Eagles.

Q: Many American White Pelicans live in the park because they like the shallow waters of Albert Lea Lake. What do white pelicans eat?

White pelicans eat fish.

THINGS TO DO IN THE AREA

Pelican Breeze Pontoon Boat Ride, Frank Hall Park, Albert Lea; 507-383-2630. Cruise beautiful Albert Lea Lake aboard the double-decker pontoon, Pelican Breeze. The narrated tour boards at Frank Hall Park on the northwest shore of the lake June–September, Saturday and Sunday at 2pm. The kids will love the Friday night pizza cruise, soda pop included. The pizza cruise is at 6pm, reservations only. Restroom on board.

Aquatic Center, 321 James Ave, Albert Lea; 507-373-3328. Cool off at the Albert Lea Aquatic Center. The water park has 2 diving platforms, a 226-foot slide, kiddie splash pool and concessions. Open daily June–August,. Admission is free for children ages 2 and under.

Blazing Star Trail, (trailhead is located at Frank Hall Park), Albert Lea. Blazing Star is currently 6.5 miles of paved biking/hiking trail with a special emphasis on pristine wetlands. There are plans in the works to join Blazing Star with the Shooting Star Trail for a ride from Albert Lea to the Mississippi River.

DINING

Bunnell's Donut Hut, 1220 E Main (corner of Hwy 65 & Garfield's), Albert Lea; 507-373-5770. The full-time bakery not only offers all the wonderful mouth-watering treats everyone loves, but also makes sandwiches-to-go for picnics. **Lakeside Café & Creamery**, 408 Bridge Ave, Albert Lea; 507-377-2233. Sandwiches, soups and hand-dipped ice cream cones. **The Trumble's**, 1811 E Main, Albert Lea; 507-373-2638. Not fancy, just good food with a family atmosphere. Their specialties are fresh baked pies and cinnamon rolls. Open daily. **Tail Fins**, (exit 146, I-90), Alden; 507-874-3775; www.tailfins-maltshop.com. Malt shop and ice cream parlor, '50s style!

LODGING

AmericInn, 811 East Plaza (exit 157, I-90), Albert Lea; 800-634-3444 or 507-373-4324; www.americinn.com. Free continental breakfast, indoor pool and spa, game room. **Bel-Aire Motor Inn**, (exit 154, I-90), Albert Lea; 800-373-4073 or 507-373-3983. Outdoor pool, free continental breakfast; kids ages 14 and under stay free. **Comfort Inn**, 810 Happy Trails Lane (I-35 at Trail's Travel Center), Albert Lea; 507-377-1100. Indoor pool and free continental breakfast. **Country Inn & Suites**, 2214 E Main Street, Albert Lea; 800-456-4000 or 507-

373-5513; www.countryinns.com/albertleamn. Indoor pool and spa, exercise room and free continental breakfast. Days Inn, 2301 E Main Street (I-35, exit 11 or 12), Albert Lea; 800-218-2989 or 507-373-8291. Indoor pool, restaurant and game room. Holiday Inn Express, 821 Plaza Street (exit 157, I-90), Albert Lea; 800-HOLIDAY or 507-373-4000. Indoor pool and free continental breakfast. Ramada of Albert Lea, 23056 E Main Street (I-35, exits 11 or 12), Albert Lea; 866-373-6471 or 507-373-6471; www.ramadaalbertlea.com. Indoor pool and restaurant.

CAMPING

Myre-Big Island State Park, located 3 miles southeast of town at the south end of Cty 38, Albert Lea; 507-379-3403. Hiking, fishing, picnic shelter, canoe rental, snowmobiling, skiing, 100 campsites (32 with electricity) and a camper cabin that sleeps 5. KOA Kampground, Hayward; 507-373-5170. Playground, game room, 9-hole golf course and driving range, horseshoes, camp store, camp cabins. Public pool is open daily. Admission charged. Hickory Hills Campgrounds, located 7 miles south of Albert Lea on Hwy 69 S; 507-852-4555; www.hickoryhillscampground.com. 90 campsites. Outdoor pool, basketball court, camp store, game room, horseshoes, volleyball, softball, mini golf, hiking and skiing. Open year-round.

MORE STUFF

Albert Lea Convention & Visitors Bureau, 143 W Clark Street, Albert Lea; 800-345-8414 or 507-373-3938; www.albertleatourism.org. City of Albert Lea Parks & Recreation Department, 221 E Clark Street, Albert Lea; 507-377-4370. Cinema 7 Theatre, Northbridge Mall, 2510 Bridge Ave (I-90 & Bridge Ave), Albert Lea; 507-373-7039. Myre-Big Island State Park, 507-379-3403. Canoe rental.

Lily pads

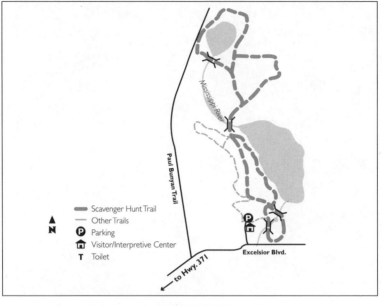

On the west side of Brainerd; 218-829-8770

Scavenger Hunt Trail
Other Trails
P Parking
Visitor/Interpretive Center
T Toilet

Mississippi River

Paul Bunyan Trail

N

Excelsior Blvd.

to Hwy. 371

NORTHLAND ARBORETUM

POINTS OF INTEREST:
Beautiful gardens, beaver ponds, red pine forest

TOTAL TRAIL MILES: 12.5
THIS HIKE: 2 miles
DIFFICULTY: Easy to moderate
ELEVATION: 70 feet

The 540-acre Northland Arboretum is an untamed natural beauty, enhanced in areas with fragrant gardens and walking paths. It is the perfect place to learn about Jack pines (the arboretum is home to one of the few stands left in the state) and wildlife such as beavers, white-tailed deer, black bear, 41 species of butterflies and 63 species of birds. An on-site, 40-acre former landfill (now mostly grassland) offers the unique opportunity to discuss ecological man-made problems and solutions with the kids.

The Northland Arboretum has 12.5 miles of trails with an elevation gain of 70 feet. The trail circling a replica of Monet's garden is close to the restrooms and an ideal spot for a picnic. The other trails are gently rolling, very scenic hikes through the woods. The trails are well marked, but the grass does get a bit thick and long in sections and is not stroller friendly. There are interpretive signs along the Big Ben Trail.

WHERE TO BEGIN

The Northland Arboretum is located between the towns of Baxter and Brainerd, along the Paul Bunyan State Bike Trail. From Hwy 371, turn east (right) on Hwy 210 in Baxter, drive toward Brainerd and the Mississippi River. Take a left (north) on Baxter Dr and follow to Excelsior Rd; take a left (west) and watch for the arboretum entrance on the right. Park in the lot by the visitor center and pick up a trail map.

The visitor center is open year-round, Monday–Friday; the restroom is open daily until 10pm. A small fee is charged for trail use. At the time of this writing, a formal picnic area was located in the Monet garden gazebo, but plans were underway to expand picnic sites. Another restroom facility is near the gazebo area. In the winter, the arboretum grooms over 12 miles of lighted cross-country ski and snowshoe trails through a picturesque forest. Classes offered throughout the year include planting and growing your own pumpkins on-site, birdhouse building and maintenance, proper use of a compass and cross-country ski lessons.

THE TRAILS

Big Ben, Johnson, North Star & Little Ben Trails (scavenger hunt)
The 2-mile loop begins at the parking lot at Monet's Garden. After exploring the gardens and wetland habitat, hike the Big Ben ridge, a rolling trail with interesting views of a deep ravine and pond. The Jack pine savanna is located at the convergence of several trails; this is also a great place to be on the lookout for beaver lodges and dams. Head northeast on the Johnson Trail around the Red Pine Plantation. The height of these magnificent trees is truly awe inspiring. Take the quick North Star loop for a bird's-eye view of several beaver ponds, then head back to the parking lot on Little Ben, another ridge hike that cuts through beautiful woods of mostly maples and oaks.

Potlatch, Acorn & South Acorn Trails Park in the gravel lot behind the maintenance building and begin the 1.5-mile loop on South Acorn, a grassy trail that skirts the landfill and connects with Acorn and Potlatch Trails. The Paul Bunyan State Bike Trail runs parallel to the hike along the west side. Return to the parking lot along Little Ben or Rudy's. This scenic hike through woods and grassland is gently rolling, but could get a bit long for kids under 6 years old.

SCAVENGER HUNT Big Ben, Johnson, North Star & Little Ben Trails

1. Bridge over pond

2. Gazebo gardens

3. Bird house

4. Emerson rock

5. Rock wall garden

6. White pines

7. Tree nodules where there was once a branch

8. Trail sign

9. Deer hoof print

10. Stream that runs under the trail

11. Tree farm area

12. Red pine

13. Beaver pond

TRIVIA QUESTIONS

Q: There are lots of beavers living in the marshes of the Northland Arboretum. What is a beaver home called?

Beavers live in a self-made structure called a "lodge." This tepee-like mound of tangled sticks plastered with mud is strongly reinforced. It is nearly impossible for even the powerful black bear to break it.

Q: Beavers love the water and can swim as fast as 6 mph. How long can they hold their breath underwater?

Beavers can hold their breath underwater for up to 15 minutes.

Q: Conservationists sometimes light fires in the Northland Arboretum in what is called a "controlled burn." What are some of the natural benefits of this process?

Some of the benefits of a controlled forest fire include killing the non-native plant species to make way for the native plants. A carefully planned fire also burns all the dead forest undergrowth known as "fuel," which then makes the threat of a wildfire less dangerous.

Q: What pine tree needs fire in order to reseed itself?

The pine cones of the Jack pine are sealed by a heat-sensitive resin and will not open and release their seeds without fire. The Northland Arboretum has a beautiful example of a Jack pine savanna.

Q: Fishing is a very popular area attraction. What are some of the common fish found in Northern Minnesota?

Some common fish of the north include walleyes (the state fish), saugers, northern pike, muskellunge, largemouth bass, smallmouth bass, black crappies, white crappies, pumpkin-seed, bluegills and green sunfish.

THINGS TO DO IN THE AREA

Paul Bunyan Land, Hwy 18 (located 7 miles east of town), Brainerd; 218-764-2524; www.ThisOldFarm.net. Everyone needs to meet Paul Bunyan, Minnesota's celeb lumberjack. Paul truly is larger than life and so are his tall tales. Head to Paul Bunyan Land for an up-close and personal chat with the big guy, then turn the kids loose on all the rides the theme park offers, which includes an arcade and petting farm. Open Memorial Day–Labor Day. Old Farm Pioneer Village and concessions. Admission fee charged; free for ages 2 and under.

Paul Bunyan Nature Learning Center, 7187 Wise Rd, Brainerd; 218-829-9620; www.lakesarea.net. The Paul Bunyan Nature Learning Center is one cool place you and the kids will love. The emphasis is on conservation and sharing knowledge through hands-on, naturalist-led programs. More than 3 miles of trails hike through both woods and wetlands. The nature center is completely geared to kids with lots of feel-and-touch type exhibits. Open year-round; free admission.

Cuyuna State Recreation Area, 307 3rd Street (15 miles northeast of Brainerd on Hwy 210), Ironton; 218-546-5926. Cuyuna Rec Area is 5,000 pristine acres of mostly undeveloped wilderness. Scuba dive the crystal clear waters of the abandoned mine pit lakes, canoe, fish for trout, hike, camp and watch for Bald Eagles.

Croft Mine Historical Park, N 8th Street & 2nd Ave E, Crosby; 218-546-5466. The 17-acre park features historic buildings and mining artifacts from the early 1900s, when the Merrimac Mining Company was operating in full swing. The guided tour includes simulated underground ore mining. Open daily, Memorial Day–Labor Day. Fee charged; children younger than kindergarten are free.

Nisswa Turtle Races, Main Street (downtown, behind the Chamber of Commerce), Nisswa; 218-963-2620. Rent a painted turtle or bring your own to the Nisswa turtle races held every Wednesday at 2pm. For more than 40 years, June–August, the town has been cheering on the champs all the way to the finish line. Small entrance fee; cash prizes awarded.

Paul Bunyan State Bike Trail. At a whopping 210 miles long, the Paul Bunyan State Bike Trail is the longest converted rails-to-trails system in North America. It wouldn't seem right if something with Paul's name on it wasn't the longest. Bike, hike, in-line skate and snowmobile the trail that begins off of Hwy 210 between Baxter and Brainerd. Check out the website for all the details. www.paulbunyantrail.com.

Scheer's Lumberjack Shows, located 1 block south of Jct of Hwy 371 & Cty 16, 2 miles north of Pequot Lakes; 218-568-5997 or 715-634-6923; www.scheerslumberjackshow.com. Watch the hilarious and incredibly skilled lumberjack athletes compete in ten different events including pole climbing, axe throwing, log rolling and cross-cut sawing. AND they can pull off plaid, so there you go. Memorial Day–Labor Day; no shows on Sunday or Monday. Admission charged.

The Minnesota Fishing Museum, 304 W Broadway, Little Falls; 320-616-2011; www.mnfishingmuseum.com. Before you go fishing with the kids, take them to the Minnesota Fishing Museum for a look at the trophy fish you'll have them casting for. The museum's two showrooms house over 7,000 artifacts, boat and motor displays and a 1920s fishing and hunting cabin. The museum is open year-round; closed on Mondays (closed Sundays and Mondays during the winter). Admission is free for children ages 9 and under; free for everyone on Tuesdays.

Charles A. Lindbergh Historic Site, 1620 Lindbergh Dr S, Little Falls; 888-727-8386 or 320-616-5421. Charles Lindbergh was the first person to fly across the Atlantic Ocean alone. As a boy, Lindbergh spent his summers in Little Falls. The 1906 family home has many of its original furnishings. The visitor center also features original film footage of the famous flight and a full-scale replica of Lindbergh's plane—the Spirit of St. Louis. Open daily Memorial Day–Labor Day, closed Mondays. Admission charged.

DINING

371 Diner, Edgewood Dr (on the frontage road), Baxter; 218-829-3356. The 50s-style restaurant serves kids' meals in little old-fashioned cars. Fun family atmosphere, malts, full menu and all-day breakfast. Open daily, year-round. Rafferty's Pizza, 14136 Baxter Dr (located in the Westgate Mall), Baxter; 218-829-5804. Sure, Rafferty's has pizza, but they've also got chicken, burgers, sandwiches and 18 flavors of Bridgeman's ice cream! Open year-round. Dave's Pizza, Hwy 371 N, Baxter; 218-824-2000. Dave's has nearly every kind of pizza imaginable, along with soups and specialty sandwiches. Also a kids' menu and ice cream. Open daily, year-round. Poncho and Lefty's, Hwy 371, Baxter; 218-829-0489. Open year-round for lunch and dinner, Poncho and Lefty's offers Mexican dining with an emphasis on a family-friendly, casual atmosphere.

LODGING

AmericInn, Hwy 371 & Cty 16 (2 miles north of Pequot Lakes on Hwy 371); 888-568-8400 or 218-568-8400; www.upnorthlodge.com. Indoor pool and spa, free breakfast buffet, playground, mini golf, volleyball court, shuffleboard, outdoor Ping-pong and horseshoes, rec room and on-site pizza. Holiday Inn Express, Hwy 371 N, Baxter; 218-824-3232. "Kids Cabins" and a large indoor Three Bear Lodge Water and Theme Park with 3 slides, a lazy river, hot tubs, activity pool, game room and concessions. Rapid River Lodge & Waterpark, Comfort Suites, 7376 Wolda Rd, Baxter; 877-543-8938 or 218-825-7234. Indoor water park with 2 giant slides, a lazy river and a kiddie pool with a tree fort, indoor/outdoor sauna and Jacuzzi, game room, concessions, free deluxe continental breakfast. Hawthorn Inn & Suites, 7208 Fairview Rd, Baxter; 800-527-1133 or 218-822-1133; www.hawthorn.com. Indoor pool, spa and kiddie pool, game room, outdoor pool with gas grills, free hot breakfast buffet and convenience store. Ramada Inn, 2115 S 6th Street (business Hwy 371 N), Brainerd; 218-829-1441; www.ramadamn.com. Indoor pool and spa, game room, tennis court and on-site restaurant. Country Inn, 23884 Front Street, Deerwood; 800-456-4000 or 218-534-3101. Indoor pool and spa, free continental breakfast. Breezy Point, 9252 Breezy Point Dr, Breezy Point; 800-432-3777; www.breezypointresort.com. Famous for their world-class golf courses, Breezy Point won't disappoint in the family fun department either. Located on beautiful Pelican Lake, the resort has kids' programs, arts & crafts, swimming pools, a gorgeous sand beach, games, movies, great fishing, an ice arena, tennis courts, kayaks, canoes, paddleboats, hydro-bikes, pontoons, fishing boats and fishing guides, disc golf and 2 restaurants. Cragun's, 11000 Craguns Dr, Brainerd; 800-272-4867 or 218-825-2700; www.craguns.com. It would almost be easier to list what they don't have at Cragun's, because let me tell you, this place has it all: family fun nights, kids' programs, nature hikes, basketball, volleyball, tennis, biking, arts & crafts, games, scavenger hunts, spa, water-skiing, waterslide and swimming pools, indoor sports center, guided fishing trips, canoeing, pontoon and boat rentals, downhill and cross-country skiing, snowmobile and Kitty Kat rentals, ice skating, dog sled and horse-drawn trolley rides, golf course and 5 restaurants.

CAMPING

Don & Mayva's Crow Wing Lake Campground, 2393 Crow Wing Camp Rd, Brainerd; 218-829-6468; www.crowwingcamp.com. 100 campsites with hookups, camp store, heated outdoor pool, large playground, Frisbee golf, rec room, bank shot basketball, fishing, hiking, volleyball and boat, canoe and paddleboat rentals. Sullivan's Resort & Campground, 7685 Cty 127, Brainerd; 888-829-5697; www.sullivansresort.com. 50 campsites with hookups. Sandy beach, heated indoor pool and spa, camp store, boat, motor and pontoon rentals, excellent fishing. Galles' Upper Cullen Campground, Nisswa; 888-872-8553; www.uppercullen.com. 50 campsites, some with hookups. Sandy beach and playground, free hayrides, hiking, petting zoo, camp store, rec room, boat, motor, pontoon and paddleboat rentals. Highview Campground & RV Park, 11090 Old Cty 39, Breezy Point; 218-543-4526. 100 campsites with hookups, rec room, playground, camp store, sand swimming beach, boat, motor and canoe rentals, fishing.

MORE STUFF

Brainerd Lakes Area Chambers of Commerce, 7393 Hwy 371 (located 7 miles south of Brainerd-Baxter), Brainerd 56401; 800-450-2838 or 218-829-2838; www.explorebrainerdlakes.com. Crosslake Chamber (located at the corner of Cty 3 & 66), 218-692-1828. Pequot Lakes Chamber (located downtown), 800-950-0291 or 218-568-8911. Trailblazer Bikes, Brainerd; 218-829-8542. Bike rental and shuttle service. Cycle Path & Paddle, Crosby; 218-545-4545. Bike, canoe and kayak rentals. Cross-country ski and snowshoe rentals. Easy Riders Bicycle & Sports Shop (and museum), Brainerd; 218-829-5516. Bike, in-line skate, canoe and kayak rentals; shuttle service. Ice skate rentals. Easy Riders is also a museum that houses 100 antique bikes and toys. Open daily, except Sundays; free admission. Cragun's Resort, Brainerd; 218-825-2700; www.craguns.com. Bike, canoe, fishing, pontoon, sail and ski boat rentals.

Breezy Point Resort, Breezy Point; 218-562-7811; www.breezypointresort.com. Bike, canoe, fishing and pontoon rentals. Personal watercraft rentals. Snow tubing. Dave's Sportland Rental, Hwy 371 & Cty 13, Nisswa; 218-963-2401; www.davessportland.com. Jet Ski, ski boat, tube, kneeboard, ski, wakeboard and pontoon rentals. Bait & tackle; fishing guides. Crystal-Pierz Rentals, Gull Lake; 218-963-1010 or 218-963-7788; www.crystalpierz.com. Fishing, ski and pontoon rentals. Royal's Fishing Guide Service, 800-366-8315 or 218-829-6672 (cell 218-821-5400); www.brainerdfishing-guide.com. BoardSports U.S.A., 14039 Edgewood Dr, Baxter; 866-502-8200; www.boardsportsusa.com. Kite board rentals and lessons. Ski Gull, Cty 77/Pine Beach Rd (located on the west side of Gull Lake); 218-963-4353; www.skigull.com. Downhill ski and snow tubing. Rentals and lessons available. 14 runs; open Thurs–Mon (winter). Primetime Snow Tubing, located a half mile off Cty 11, Breezy Point; 218-562-6013. Little Pine Livery Co., 15024 Wilderness Trl, Crosslake; 218-692-2974. Horseback riding. Outback Trail Rides, Inc., 12210 Pillsbury Forest Rd SW, Pillager; 218-746-3990. Horseback riding; hay& sleigh rides. Pine River Riding Stable, Hwy 371 N to Cty 2W, Pine River; 218-587-5807. Horseback riding, hay rides, petting zoo and picnic area. Benvelle Equestrian Center, 4828 Tree Farm Rd, Pequot Lakes; 218-568-4826; www.benvelleequestriancenter.com. Horseback riding. Minnesota School of Diving, 712 Washington Street, Brainerd; 218-829-5953. Scuba gear rentals. Movies 10 Westgate, 1180 Excelsior Rd, Baxter; 218-828-6228. Brainerdgolftrail.com. This website features the top golf courses in the region. Pirates Cove Adventure Golf, 17992 Hwy 371 N, Brainerd; 218-828-9002. 18-hole mini golf. Kart Kountry, 17568 Hwy 371 N, Brainerd; 218-829-4963; www.kartkountry.com. Fun park with Go-Karts, bumper boats, mini golf, batting cages, arcade and water wars. Open Memorial Day–Labor Day; pay-as-you-play. Wildwedge, Hwy 371, 2 miles north of Pequot Lakes (next to AmericInn); 218-568-6995; www.wildwedge.com. Par 3 golf and 18-hole mini golf; concessions. Bump N Putt, Hwy 371 (1 mile south of Pequot Lakes); 218-568-8833. Fun park with water wars, mini golf, landrovers, play maze, games, concessions. Whistling Wolf Mini-Golf and Gifts, 36006 Cty 66, Crosslake; 218-692-4653. 18-hole mini golf and surrey bike rentals. Civic Center, 218-828-2320. Indoor ice skating arena. Beaver Dam Ballooning, 218-838-6191. Hot air balloon rides over the Brainerd Lakes area.

North of Pipestone; 507-825-5464

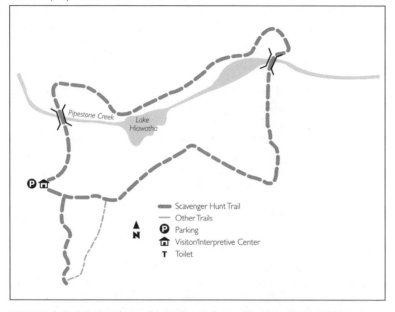

Scavenger Hunt Trail
Other Trails
P Parking
Visitor/Interpretive Center
T Toilet

PIPESTONE NATIONAL MONUMENT

POINTS OF INTEREST:
Waterfall, Pipestone Quarry, visitor center

TOTAL TRAIL MILES: 1
THIS HIKE: 1-mile loop
DIFFICULTY: Easy
ELEVATION: 30 feet

The grounds of Pipestone National Monument are sacred to the Native American culture. For centuries, Native Americans traveled to Pipestone to quarry the red stone found there. The stone is called catlinite, or pipestone, and it is used to make peace pipes and other ceremonial items. Quarrying the pipestone is hard, tedious work. Using only hand tools, the quarrier must break through 10–15 feet of Sioux Quartzite, which is harder than steel, to get to the soft, red pipestone. As you walk the trail, you might notice bits of colored cloth tied to sticks and trees or small pouches of tobacco or sage. These are traditional Native American symbols or prayers of gratitude for the pipestone and all needs provided by Mother Earth. Please do not disturb these gifts.

Pipestone National Monument has one trail—a 1-mile loop with an elevation gain of 30 feet at the waterfall. It is an easy, interesting interpretive trail that follows the Pipestone Creek through the woods to the falls, then cuts through open prairie to the pipestone quarries.

WHERE TO BEGIN

Pipestone National Monument is located at the southwestern corner of the state, 1 mile north of Pipestone on Hwy 75; www.nps.gov/pipe/. There is a small entrance fee payable at the visitor center.

The center has a great interpretive area showcasing types of pipestone, carved peace pipes, educational videos and a slide program shown every half hour. It also has a gift shop, restrooms, drinking water and a display area where you can view people carving the pipestone. Pick up a trail map and Circle Trail Worksheet for the kids at the front desk. The worksheet has all kinds of fun facts, trivia and scavenger hunt items.

THE TRAILS

Circle Trail The easy 1-mile loop begins through a door accessed from inside the visitor center. There are more than 300 plant species living in this habitat, but 200 years ago that wasn't the case, when this ground was covered primarily in grass. Follow the river past the Spotted Pipestone Quarry and through the woods. Be on the lookout for Great Blue Heron (mostly gray colored). They frequently stand along the marshy edge, hunting for fish. As you approach the 30-foot Winnewissa Falls, you'll see a natural rock formation of what looks like an old man's face. The trail splits here. The stairs lead up to the top of the falls, then join again with the trail through the small canyon, or you can cross the bridge and enter the canyon. Watch the toddlers around the falls, as much of the area is without guardrails. The trail is stroller friendly up to the falls, but gets a bit rough as it leads through the canyon area. Another fun side trail is a climb to the top of the cliff for a look at the Oracle, another natural rock formation of a face that the old tribal shamans believed could talk. As you hike out of the woods, notice the undisturbed tallgrass prairie; it is much the same as it was centuries ago. Continue the loop to the pipestone quarries, still active today. The trail ends at the nature center, where you'll see a quarry pit opened for your exploration.

SCAVENGER HUNT (Circle Trail)

1. Striped stone

2. Great Blue Heron

3. Old Stone Face

4. Rippled stone

5. 1838 Nicollet Expedition commemorative plaque

6. Inscription Rock—Pioneer names carved in rock

7. The Oracle

8. Sioux Quartzite layers (it is harder than ordinary steel)

9. Native American gift to Mother Earth

10. Pipestone quarry

TRIVIA QUESTIONS

Q: Why do some stones have rippled marks?

This area was once part of an ancient sand beach. The wave action of the ancient sea left ripple marks on the sand. When the sand became stone, the ripple marks stayed.

Q: The falls are named Winnewissa. What does the word "Winnewissa" mean?

"Winnewissa" is the Dakota Indian word for "jealous maiden."

Q: What was one way the young Native Americans proved their bravery?

Young Indian warriors used to jump from one rock tower to another.

Q: In 1838, Joseph Nicollet explored the pipestone quarries and surrounding areas. Who was Joseph Nicollet?

> *Joseph Nicollet was a brilliant French mathematician and scientist. He was the first to lead a United States government expedition through the quarries. He also created the first accurate map of the Upper Mississippi region, including Minnesota.*

Q: Native Americans still quarry the red pipestone today. What is pipestone and what is it used for?

> *Pipestone is a relatively soft clay, comparable to the hardness of your fingernail. It is used to make ceremonial pipes such as the peace pipe, but also is used for personal ornaments and ceremonial tablets.*

THINGS TO DO IN THE AREA

Blue Mounds State Park, 1410 161st Street (3 miles from Luverne, drive north 4 miles on Hwy 75; turn east on Cty 20 for 1 mile to park entrance), Luverne; 507-283-1307. The 2,028-acre park claims several unusual features: it is home to the prickly pear cactus (blooms June & July), a herd of buffalo and an unexplained 1,250-foot line of ancient rocks that aligns with the sun on the first day of spring and the first day of fall. It also has a nice swimming beach, 1,500 acres of 7-foot-high prairie grasslands, rock climbing, 13 miles of hiking trails, fishing, canoe rentals and a 100-foot-high ridge of Sioux Quartzite that appeared blue to the pioneers as they journeyed west, thus the park's namesake. By the way, early morning is the best time to view the buffalo from the observation platform. Open year-round.

Prairie Heights Bison, 1541 Hwy 75 (3.5 miles north of Luverne on Hwy 75), Luverne; 507-283-8136; www.buybison.com. Did you know bison can run up to 45 mph? And did you know the hump on a bison's back keeps it from turning over? Take a guided wagon tour through a bison herd and learn all about these mighty animals. After you feed the bison, the folks at Prairie Heights will feed you lemonade and cookies. Grilled cookouts and BBQs available on request. Day and evening tours run May–Labor Day; call for reservations. Fee charged; children ages 4 and under free with paid adult.

Song of Hiawatha Pageant, adjacent to the Pipestone National Monument, 800-430-4126 or 507-825-4126; www.pipestoneminnesota.com/pageant/. Annually since 1949, the residents of Pipestone have presented live performances of the Hiawatha Pageant, a story based on Henry Wadsworth Longfellow's 1853 poem about an Ojibwa warrior. The outdoor amphitheater includes the sacred grounds of the Three Maidens—six large granite boulders thought to be the fragments of.one gigantic boulder leftover from the last Ice Age 10,000 years ago. The play is performed the last two weekends in July and the first weekend in August (Fri, Sat & Sun). The grounds are open to the public at 6pm; the play begins at sundown around 9:15pm. Concessions and restrooms on premises; fee charged; children ages 10 and under are free with a paying adult.

Pipestone Family Aquatic Center, located at the Jct of Hwys 23, 30 & 75; 507-825-7946 or 507-825-5834. The older kids will love the aquatic center's flume waterslide and diving board; the tots will have fun in their own water and sand play area. The center also has sand volleyball courts and a nearby playground and picnic area. Open daily throughout the summer. Fee charged.

McCone Sod Houses, 12598 Magnolia Ave (20 miles east of Walnut Grove), Sanborn; 507-723-5138. The McCone Sod Houses are a bit of a drive from Pipestone, but worth the miles if you want the kids to get a real glimpse of pioneer life on the prairie. Self-guided tours hike through a sea of 8-foot tall-grass to two full-sized sod house replicas authentically furnished in the 1880s period. Two-foot-thick dirt walls, a dirt floor, dried grass roof, plain furniture and an outhouse provide the feel for the hardships faced by the homesteaders. You can stay the night in one of the houses and experience for yourself what it was like to live in the days without running water or electricity. The McCone Sod Houses are open daily, Apr–Oct. Small admission charge; children ages 6 and under are free. Call for an overnight reservation.

DINING

Lange's Cafe & Bakery, Hwys 23 & 75, Pipestone; 507-825-4488. Full menu of home cooking, including pastries and bread. Breakfast served all day long. Lange's is famous for its caramel rolls and sour cream raisin pie. Open 24 hours daily. Villager Restaurant, Hwy 75 N, Pipestone; 507-825-5242. Full menu includes breakfast, sandwiches, Mexican fare, broasted chicken and six flavors of ice cream. Kids' menu. Open daily at 6am. Dar's Pizza, located at the corner of 8th Ave SW & Hwy 30, Pipestone; 507-825-4261. Pizza, sandwiches, chicken and shrimp. Game room. Open daily at 4pm.

LODGING

AmericInn Lodge & Suites, 1475 Darling Dr, Worthington; 800-634-3444 or 507-376-4500; www.americinn.com. Indoor pool and spa, free continental breakfast with waffles, adjacent restaurant. Days Inn, 207 Oxford Street, Worthington; 800-329-7466 or 507-376-6155. Indoor pool and spa, free continental breakfast. Holiday Inn Express Hotel & Suites, 1250 Ryan's Rd, Worthington; 800-225-8825 or 507-372-2333; www.hiexpress.com/worthingtonmn. Pool and spa, game room, free deluxe continental breakfast. Adjacent restaurant and bar. Super 8 Motel, 605 8th Ave SE, Pipestone; 800-800-8000 or 507-825-4217. Cribs and rollaways available. Adjacent restaurant. Travelodge Hotel, 2015 Humiston Ave N, Worthington; 507-372-2991; www.travelodge.com. Indoor pool, free continental breakfast for two. On-site restaurant and lounge.

CAMPING

Pipestone RV Campground, 919 Hiawatha Ave N. (across from Pipestone National Monument & Hiawatha Pageant grounds), Pipestone; 507-825-2455; www.pipestonervcampground.com. Large campground with full hookups and 13 tent sites, group camping, 2 tepees. Heated pool, ice cream, gift shop, playground. Open mid-Apr–Oct. Split Rock Creek State Park, 336 50th Ave (located 7 miles south of Pipestone off of Hwy 23), Jasper; 507-348-7908. 28 campsites (19 electric), 6 tent sites. Split Rock Creek is situated on the largest lake in Pipestone County. Nice swimming beach, fishing, 4.5 miles of hiking trails and a Sioux Quartzite stone dam. Open year-round. Blue Mounds State Park, 1410 161st Street, Luverne 56156; 507-283-1307. 73 campsites (40 electric), 14 tent sites. Rock climbing, 13 miles of hiking trails, canoe rental, swimming and a buffalo herd. Open year-round; park office has maps and nature store. Olson Park Campground, PO Box 279 (from I-90, drive south on 266 to Cty 35, then west 1 mile to Cty 10; drive south 2 miles), Worthington; 507-372-8650; www.ci.worthington.mn.us/pw%20parks.htm. 61 campsites (57 electric), hiking, swimming, playground, boat dock. Open Apr–Oct.

MORE STUFF

Pipestone Area Chamber and Visitors Bureau, 117 8th Ave SE, Pipestone 56164; 800-336-6125 or 507-825-3316; www.pipestoneminnesota.com. Luverne Chamber of Commerce, 102 E Main, Luverne 56156; 507-283-4061. Worthington Area Convention & Visitors Bureau, 1121 3rd Ave, Worthington 56187; 800-279-2919 or 507-372-2919; www.worthingtonmnchamber.com. Travel Southwest Minnesota, 866-609-7673; www.travelsw.org. Information about area attractions, lodging and camping. Blue Mounds State Park, 1410 161st Street, Luverne; 507-283-1307. Canoe rental beginning Memorial weekend. Quarry Twin Theater, 204 E Main Street, Pipestone; 507-825-3522. Northland Cinema 5, 1635 Oxford Street, Worthington; 507-376-4400. Palace Theatre, 205 N Freeman Ave, Luverne; 507-283-8294.

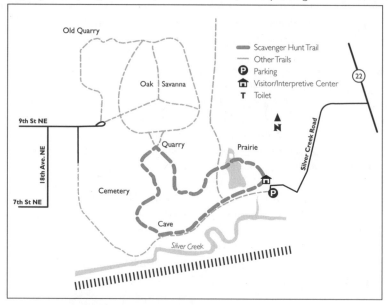

QUARRY HILL PARK

POINTS OF INTEREST:
Nature center, fishing pond, old quarry, caves, fossils

TOTAL TRAIL MILES: 5
THIS HIKE: 1 mile
DIFFICULTY: Easy
ELEVATION: 80 feet

Easy, interesting hiking trails and an awesome nature center make this park a real favorite. Quarry Hill has tons of things to do. An old limestone retaining wall is a great place to practice your rock climbing skills. Kids ages 15 and under can drop a line and try their luck in the 2-acre fishing pond (ages 16 and over must have a fishing license; bring your own gear and bait). A paved bike path through the woods connects the park with the 60-mile Rochester bike system. Examine the fossils in the prehistoric limestone quarry or take a tour through one of the sandstone caves. Tours are given on the third Sunday of each month. Bring your own flashlight. A small admission is charged.

Quarry Hill Park has 5 miles of trails with an elevation gain of 80 feet. The trails loop a wooded hillside, an old quarry with 350-million-year-old fossils, an oak savanna, a bog, caves, a cemetery, pond, stream and prairie. Quarry Hill Park really does have it all!

WHERE TO BEGIN

Quarry Hill Park is at 701 Silver Creek Rd NE. There are two easy ways to find the park: from Broadway (downtown), take 4th Street SE and turn left onto Cty 22 and watch for the sign or take 14th Street NE and turn right onto Cty 22.

Begin your adventure with a trip through the awesome Nature Center. Fossils, snakeskins and animal furs are placed at stroller height for little fingers. Aquariums house native fish, turtles, frogs, snakes and other creepy crawlers. Through a glass wall, watch busy bees build a honeycomb and attend their queen. Do some backyard bird watching—Quarry Hill supplies the binoculars and bird books. Have a look at the life-sized replica of a T-Rex skull or learn about fossils and nature in the children's library. Quarry Hill Nature Center has over 100 mounted animals, a real 4-foot-long dinosaur femur, stroller-friendly aisles, restrooms, information, trail maps, drinking water and cross-country ski and snowshoe rental. Open daily, year-round. Free admission.

NOTE: For a nominal fee, Quarry Hill offers a variety of nature programs including full moon hikes, canoeing, rock climbing and more.

THE TRAILS

Cave/Quarry Loop The cave/quarry hike is a 1-mile loop across the fishing pond, up a wooded trail past the remains of old quarry equipment and the quarry itself (prime fossil hunting grounds!), across a footbridge spanning a ravine that leads to a grassy knoll, cemetery, the caves, a fireplace and retaining wall. This is a great trail for kids 6 and older. The short ascent to the quarry gets a bit steep and there are a few unprotected drop-offs (especially around the quarry), but overall it's a very enjoyable hike with plenty of interesting things to explore. NOTE: Part of this trail skirts the woods along the blacktop bike trail, which is level and perfect for those with young children in strollers.

Meadow Loop The 1-mile hike travels through a bog and restored prairie, crosses over a stream and runs parallel to the woods. It is fairly level and nearly half of it is part of the paved bike trail. Bring a picnic lunch and continue on the bike trail to Parkwood Hills Park. The park has a nice playground and softball diamond.

Oak Savanna Trail The 1-mile Oak Savanna Trail is less traveled with lots of great opportunities for spotting wildlife like deer, rabbits and squirrels. From overhead, the trail sort of looks like a giant "peace" sign. You can pick up the trailhead from the backside of the Quarry Trail or come in from 9th Street NE. Here you'll find another playground, softball diamonds and a picnic area.

SCAVENGER HUNT (Cave/Quarry Loop)

1. Dragonfly

2. Limestone retaining wall left from the days when the area was a working quarry

3. Century-old limestone fireplace

4. Cave entrance

5. Old quarry

6. Cephalopod fossil (found on the quarry plateau)

7. The remains of an old shack where dynamite was stored. The explosive was used to mine the quarry rock

8. The remains of the rock crusher and storage bins

TRIVIA QUESTIONS

Q: The Quarry Hill caves were once used for food storage for a state hospital. What cave room has a secret passage?

The Butter Room has a secret passage.

Q: Name some creatures who make the cave their home.

Cave creatures include bats, crickets, spiders, moths, centipedes and mosquitoes.

Q: How old are the fossils found in the limestone quarry?

Most fossils found in the quarry are over 350 million years old.

Q: The cephalopod is the ancestor to what current animals?

The cephalopod is the ancestor to the octopus and squid.

Q: What do dragonflies eat?

Dragonflies eat insects like mosquitoes. A nymph is a baby dragonfly. It lives in the water and eats fish and tadpoles. It can take up to 5 years before a dragonfly becomes an adult. At that time, the nymph climbs ashore, its back splits open and the adult dragonfly crawls out.

THINGS TO DO IN THE AREA

Biking. Rochester has 60 miles of beautiful bike/in-line skate trails. For a map of the trail system, call the Rochester Park and Recreation Department at 507-281-6160 or the Department of Public Services, 507-281-6008 (there is a $1 charge). Download free maps from Rochester's website: www.ci.rochester.mn.us/departments/park/trails/index.asp.

Whitewater State Park, RR 1, Box 256 (3 miles south of Elba on Hwy 74), Altura 55910; 507-932-3007. Nearby Whitewater State Park has a swimming beach and bathhouse, a visitor center and nature store, 12 miles of hiking trails, 8 miles of cross-country ski trails, trout fishing, camping and year-round interpretive programs. Best of all—no mosquitoes! A favorite hike is the Chimney Rock Trail—a short, meandering 1-mile walk that starts out behind the nature store, then crisscrosses the shallow valley creek, culminating with a very steep 300-foot climb to an overlook at the top of a bluff affording a truly amazing view of the forested hillsides and valley below. Exercise lots of caution with the little ones. No guardrails, has plummeting drop-offs and lots of steps. This trail is not stroller friendly.

Silver Lake, 707 7th Street NE; 507-281-6179. Silver Lake has a nice playground, picnic area, restrooms, baseball, basketball and football fields, tennis courts, paddleboat and canoe rentals and an outdoor swimming pool that is open daily Jun–Aug. And one more thing—the park is home to more than 30,000 absolutely cool Canada Geese! See and feed these friendly honkers year-round.

Soldiers Field Pool, 224 Soldiers Field Dr SW (3rd Ave & 8th Street); 507-281-6180. The Soldiers Field Pool has a winding 112-foot slide, kiddie splash pool and restrooms. They are open daily Jun–Aug; admission charged. The adjacent Soldiers Field Park has fun, castle-like playground equipment, tennis courts, a picnic area, walking and bike paths, football and softball fields and an 18-hole golf course.

Foster-Arends Park, 400 NW East River Rd; 507-285-8316. Foster-Arends Park has a nice sand beach, swimming (no lifeguards), a picnic area, volleyball courts, fishing and canoe and paddleboat rentals.

Prairie Walls Climbing Gym, 4420 19th Street NW; 507-292-0511; www.prairiewalls.com. Here's a chance to practice your rock climbing skills. The indoor gym features over 9,500 square feet of challenging walls for the beginner, as well as the old pros. Open daily, admission charged.

Skyline Raceway & Waterslide, 2250 40th Street SW; 507-287-6289; www.skylineracewayroch.com. The Skyline has it all: waterslide, go-carts, 9-hole mini golf and paintball field. The 410-foot-high slide twists and turns and finally dumps you into a wading pool with a giant splash! Skyline Raceway & Waterslide is open year-round, daily noon–8pm; admission charged.

DINING

Daube's Bakery, 1310 5th Place NW; 507-289-3095; www.daubesbakery.com. Voted the best bakery in Rochester Magazine, Daube's serves up specialty sandwiches with breads made from scratch, soups, salads, quiche, pizza, croissants, ice cream and, oh yeah, baked goods! Open daily. NOTE: Second location is at 155 1st Ave SW; 507-252-8878. Chocolate Twist, 101 17th Ave NW; 507-529-2922. The name just sounds good, doesn't it? They have great hand-dipped cones and specialty chocolates. Open daily.

LODGING

Country Inn & Suites Rochester-South, 77 Wood Lake Dr SE; 800-456-4000 or 507-287-6758; www.countryinns.com. Indoor pool, spa, game room and free continental breakfast. Hampton Inn, 1755 S Broadway; 800-HAMPTON or 507-287-9050; www.hamptoninnrochester.com. Indoor whirlpool and spa, free continental breakfast. Hilton Garden Inn, 225 S Broadway; 800-445-8667 or 507-285-1234; www.rochestermn.gardeninn.com. Indoor pool and spa. Restaurant on site. Kahler Grand Hotel, 20 SW 2nd Ave; 800-533-1655 or 507-285-2700; www.kahler.com. Domed rooftop pool and 4 restaurants/lounges on site. Marriott Hotel, 101 SW 2nd Ave; 507-280-6000. Atrium with pool and spa, restaurant on site. Radisson Plaza Hotel, 150 S Broadway; 507-281-8000; www.radisson.com/rochestermn. Indoor pool and spa.

CAMPING

Lazy D Campground & Trail Rides, RR 1, Box 252 (located by Elba on Cty 39), Altura 55910; 507-932-3098. 115 campsites including hookups and primitive; one cabin. Heated pool, horseback riding, tube rental and fishing. Whitewater State Park, (3 miles south of Elba on Hwy 74), Altura; 507-932-3007. 106 campsites (47 electric), primitive group camp, camper cabin. Swimming beach and bathhouse, visitor center, 12 miles of hiking trails, 8 miles of cross-country ski trails. Open year-round.

MORE STUFF

Rochester Convention & Visitors Bureau, 111 S Broadway, Ste 301, (Centerplace Galleria), Rochester 55904-6511; 800-634-8277 or 507-288-4331. Rochester-Olmsted Recreation Center, 21 Elton Hills Dr NW; 507-281-6167. Indoor swimming and ice skating. Bikes on Wheels, 507-250-0097. Bike rentals. Delivery and pickup. NOTE: Deposit required. $250 charged to credit card, credited to customer once bike returned in good working order. Silver Lake Canoe & Paddleboats, W Silver Lake Dr; 507-282-1424. Canoe and paddleboat rentals; open daily, Memorial Day–Labor Day. Mayo Clinic General Tour, Judd Auditorium (located on the corner of 2nd Street SW & 2nd Ave); 507-284-2511. Free 90-minute tour and movie of the world renowned clinic. year-round, Mon–Fri at 10am. Rochester Water Ski Club, Fisherman's Inn, 8 Fisherman Dr NW (located on Lake Zumbro), Oronoco; 507-367-4485. Free weekly shows June–September on Wednesday nights at 7pm. Chateau Theatres, N Broadway & 37th Street, 507-536-SHOW. Cinemagic Theatres, 2170 Superior Dr NW, 507-280-0333.

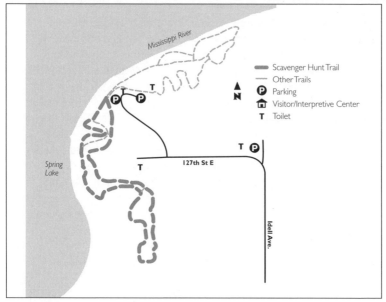

Map legend:
- Scavenger Hunt Trail
- Other Trails
- **P** Parking
- Visitor/Interpretive Center
- **T** Toilet

Mississippi River

Spring Lake

127th St E

Idell Ave.

N

SPRING LAKE PARK RESERVE & SCHAAR'S BLUFF

POINTS OF INTEREST:
Mississippi River, Bald Eagles, archery trails, model plane airfield

TOTAL TRAIL MILES: 4.87
THIS HIKE: 2.5 miles
DIFFICULTY: Easy
ELEVATION: Not a factor

Spring Lake Park is divided into three parks: Schaar's Bluff, the Archery Trail and the model plane airfield. Highlights include a huge playground, beautiful shaded picnic area overlooking the Mississippi River, volleyball, grills and two nice fire pits available on a first-come, first-served basis. The park is also popular in the winter with cross-country skiers and snowshoe enthusiasts.

The 4.87 miles of trails at Schaar's Bluff are easy and vary between grassy hikes through a restored prairie and a shaded dirt path through the woods. The wooded trail is especially beautiful, as it offers many river overlooks.

WHERE TO BEGIN

From the Twin Cities to **Schaar's Bluff**, take Hwy 52/55 south to the Hastings exit. Drive east on Hwy 55 about 4 miles, turn onto Cty 42. Follow Cty 42 east 1.8 miles to Idell Ave, drive north.

Park in the lot by the playground. Pick up a trail map here and study it while the kids have a blast on all the cool playground equipment. A paved path skirts the entire picnic area, goes over a wooden bridge and goes past two restrooms with water.

The **model plane airfield** is on the right before Schaar's Bluff on Idell Ave. There's a portable restroom in the parking lot area. The field is open summers, 8am to sunset. Permits are required.

To find the **Archery Trails**, take Hwy 52/55 south from the Twin Cities. Drive east on Hwy 55 (Hastings exit) 3.8 miles to Pine Bend Tr, turn north and drive 1.2 miles to Fahey Ave. Go north on Fahey Ave 0.1 mile to the trailhead. There's a picnic shelter here, plus horseshoe pits, restrooms and 1.38 miles of challenging, wooded archery trails. Permit fee required; trails are closed December–April, but open for cross-country skiing.

THE TRAILS

Southwest Trail The 2.5-mile trail travels southwest from the picnic grounds. The trailhead begins at the woods where the paved path ends. It zig-zags a shallow ravine, then follows the river bluffs. The views are amazing. Many islands dot the river. Watch Bald Eagles dip and soar, riding the air currents. Tugboats chug upriver pushing barges. Continuing onward, the trail becomes a wide grass path that leads through a whispering pine forest and out into a restored prairie.

For those with young children, the only real trail hazards are the overlooks. They are 200-foot limestone cliffs without guardrails, so hang on tight to your tykes.

Northeast Trail The 2-mile trail heads northeast of the playground area. It weaves past the sand volleyball courts, through the restored prairie, then offers several looped options through the woods along the river. Again, watch the little ones along the bluffs.

SCAVENGER HUNT (Southwest Trail)

1. Wooden footbridge

2. Oak burl

3. Cool boulder with crack

4. Pine cones

5. Oak leaf

TRIVIA QUESTIONS

Q: The big round lump or outgrowth you sometimes see on trees is called a burl. How is a burl formed?

A burl begins life as a gall, which is a tumor caused by insects, bacteria or fungi. The gall grows to become a burl. Burls grow with the tree, building new growth rings just like the tree. However, if you sliced open a burl you'd find the rings are usually wavy and spaced farther apart. Furniture makers love the unique look of burls and use them for all kinds of products including tables, dressers, desktops and more. Burls pose no real danger to trees.

Q: There are all kinds of red and green buoys on the river. What do they do?

The Mississippi River is like a road for tugboats pushing barges filled with coal, gravel and other goods. The buoys keep the tugboats on the safe path away from dangerous rocks and sandbars.

Q: The word Mississippi is derived from the word "Misiziibi." What does "Misiziibi" mean?

"Misiziibi" is a Native American word from the Algonquin people that means "a river spread over a large area."

Q: The river is at one of its widest points in the state at Spring Lake Park. How far is it across the river to the other shore?

It is 1 mile across to the other shore.

Q: Lots of Bald Eagles live in the Mississippi River valley. The bluffs are great for nesting and the river provides plenty of fish—the main staple in an eagle's diet. An adult Bald Eagle has 7,000 feathers and a wingspan of 7 feet. Who is bigger—the male or the female eagle?

The female Bald Eagle is bigger than the male by 30 percent.

THINGS TO DO IN THE AREA

Hastings Family Aquatic Center, 901 Maple Street (located on the left side of Hwy 55 driving west), Hastings; 651-480-2392. Splash with the kids under one of the watersprays in the kiddie pool or hit the water with a trip down the giant slide. The aquatic center has lifeguards on duty, free lockers (bring your own lock) and concessions. Nearby picnic area with grills, playground and restrooms in Roadside Park. Open Jun–Aug, noon–8pm. Admission charged; free for children ages 12 months and under.

Lock & Dam No. 2, Lock & Dam Rd (located off of 2nd Street E, right side; watch for signs), Hastings; 651-437-3150. Lock & Dam No. 2 is the second in a system of 29 locks and dams on the Mississippi between Minneapolis and St. Louis. Six million gallons of river water pumps through the lock gates, raising or lowering the river level a full 12 feet. The observation platform lets you see all the action, up-close and personal. Watch as the barge crews ready the massive barges for entering the locks. Hear the rumble of the powerful tug engines as they ease the barges into place.

Vermillion Falls Park, located off Hwy 61 (south) on 21st Street E, Hastings. The Vermillion Falls is one of the town's best-kept secrets. Against a backdrop of an old limestone ravine and flour mill, the 50-foot-wide, 19-foot-high falls makes an ideal spot for a picnic. The mill is the oldest continuous flour-milling operation in Minnesota. Many great hiking trails zigzag the beautiful rocky ravine, while other tree-lined trails head across the river and past the Veterans Home. The trail to the falls and across the bridge is paved and a good one for those with children in strollers. There are a few steps down to the falls. The park also has grills, a picnic area, restrooms and drinking water. NOTE: See the remains of the original 1857 Ramsey Mill, located on E 18th Street at King Midas Lane. During its peak, it ground out 100 barrels of flour a day. Fire destroyed it in 1894, but a part of the limestone wall is still visible.

Carpenter Nature Center, 12805 St. Croix Trail, Hastings; 651-437-4359; www.carpenternaturecenter.org. The nature center was once a private estate and huge apple orchard. It now covers over 700 acres, with more than 15 miles of self-guided trails that overlook the beautiful St. Croix River. The North Loop is a mile-long paved trail featuring an old orchard and the "sugar bush," where the sap from maple trees is collected for making syrup. Carpenter's is a natural habitat for Great Blue Herons and Bald Eagles. The interpretive center has hands-on displays, live raptors, snakes and fish and mounted wildlife specimens. They offer many educational programs and naturalist-led hikes and maintain a working apple orchard. Snowshoes available for rent on winter weekends. Open year-round, daily 8–4:30. Free admission, but donations are appreciated.

Biking/Hiking/Rollerblading. Hastings has a 15-mile paved trail system that loops the city, taking in some impressive scenery—two rivers, two lakes, a bull-frog pond, the Vermillion Falls and a close-up view of the lock & dam area. Pack a picnic lunch and play awhile at one of the many parks along the way.

Little Log House Pioneer Village, 13746 220th Street E, Hastings; 651-437-2693; www.littleloghouseshow.com. Once larger than the city of St. Paul, Hastings was known for its Victorian (nineteenth century) architecture and rare Spiral Bridge (only three known to have existed in the entire world). The city has 61 buildings on the National Register—more than any other town of its size—but, unfortunately, the Spiral Bridge is no more. Torn down in 1951, a scale model exists at the Little Log House Pioneer Village, located 6 miles south of Hastings off of Hwy 61, then east 1 mile on 220th Street. The restored village opens its gate to the public annually in July for a 3-day taste of what it was like to live in the 1800s. The rest of the year it's strictly drive-by, but worth it to see the historic bridge, gorgeous flower gardens, old-time equipment and period buildings.

DINING

Emily's Bakery & Deli, 1212 Vermillion Street, Hastings; 651-437-2491 or 651-437-3338. This is a second-generation, family-owned business serving soups, deli sandwiches and scrumptious baked goods. Check out the individual almond tarts—definitely taste bud pleasers! Open daily, year-round. **Professor Java's Coffeehouse & Deli,** 202 E 2nd Street (located in Historic Downtown), Hastings; 651-438-9962. Build-your-own sandwiches, soups, salads, baked goods, ice cream, malts, shakes, hand-dipped cones and floats. Order your meal "to go" and head across the street to Levi Park on the Mississippi River. Watch the tugs maneuver the barges upriver toward St. Paul. Open daily, year-round.

LODGING

AmericInn, 2400 Vermillion Street (Hwy 61), Hastings; 800-634-3444 or 651-437-8877; www.americinn.com. Indoor pool, spa and free continental breakfast. **Country Inn & Suites,** 300 33rd Street, Hastings; 800-456-4000 or 651-437-8870; www.countryinns.com. Indoor pool, spa and free continental breakfast.

CAMPING

Greenwood Campground, 13797 190th Street E (4 miles south of Hastings on Hwy 61, then left on 190th); 651-437-5269. 91 campsites; electric hookups and primitive. Pool, playground, volleyball and horseshoes. **St. Croix Bluffs Regional Park Campground**, 10191 St. Croix Trail S (located between Afton and Hastings on Cty 21); 651-430-8240; www.co.washington.mn.us/info_for_residents. 62 campsites with electricity, 11 tent sites. Hiking, playground, horseshoes, volleyball and tennis court.

MORE STUFF

Hastings Area Chamber of Commerce & Tourism Bureau, 111 3rd Street E, Hastings 55033; 888-612-6122 or 651-437-6775; www.hastingsmn.org. **Dakota County Parks**, 1560 Hwy 55, Hastings; 651-438-4660; www.dakotacounty.net/parks. **Hastings Theatres**, 1325 S Frontage Rd, Hastings; 651-438-9700. **Cottage View Drive-In**, 9338 E Point Douglas Rd, Cottage Grove; 651-458-5965.

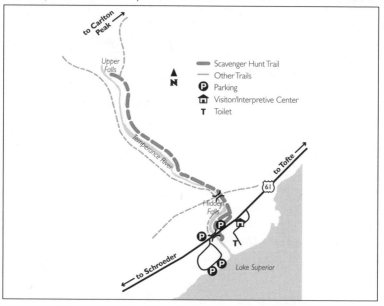

TEMPERANCE RIVER STATE PARK

POINTS OF INTEREST:
River gorge, waterfalls, potholes, ancient lava flow

TOTAL TRAIL MILES: 8
THIS HIKE: 1.75 miles (round-trip)
DIFFICULTY: Easy to moderate
ELEVATION: 240 feet

The 200-acre Temperance State Park united with the large, 2,500-acre Cross River State Wayside forming a unique park with rock cliffs, waterfalls, Lake Superior shoreline camping, the Cross and Temperance Rivers and a wicked river chasm that carved its way through a billion-year-old lava flow.

Temperance River State Park has 8 miles of hiking trails with a total elevation gain of 930 feet. The Superior Hiking Trail weaves its way along the Cross River, then veers northeast toward the Temperance River for a view of the falls and then heads north for a trek to Carlton Peak. At an elevation of 1,526 feet, the peak is one of the highest points in the region.

WHERE TO BEGIN

The park entrance is 1 mile north of Schroeder on the right side of Hwy 61. Restrooms, drinking water and trail maps are at the park office. Then back-track to Hwy 61, turn left (south) and park at the lot next to the river, where you'll find the trailhead for the Cauldron Trail.

Most of the trails within the park offer some type of challenge and can be very steep for short stretches, but the scenery is a huge gain versus any pain suffered from aching leg muscles.

THE TRAILS

Cauldron Trail The 1.75-mile (round-trip) Cauldron Trail is one of the most exciting hikes on the North Shore. A short, steep climb leads to the cascade and Hidden Falls. This is an amazing stretch of terrain. The hard basaltic rock gives way ever-so-slightly to the forces of the raging river in a deep, narrow chasm. The river funnels into the chasm as a roller coaster of whitewater rapids, then does a frantic whirl through the cauldron before dropping about 17 feet over the rock ledge on its way to Lake Superior. The water continues its cas-cade action upriver, where you'll find a 10-foot-high falls. There are dozens of unadvertised trails to the water's edge and many places for wading. You will not run out of scenic overlooks, with each more spectacular than the last.

Notice the many potholes along the trail and the stretch of pitted rock that is actually an ancient lava flow. There are lots of relatively safe viewing areas of the gorge and a cool bridge overlooking the river, but for those with young children the entire region is perilous, so exercise extreme caution. This is not a stroller-friendly trail. However, the trail across the highway to Lake Superior offers beautiful views and smooth sailing for strollers to the bridge.

Carlton Peak Trail You'll rack up 6.2 miles (round-trip) with a hike from the Hwy 61 parking lot to the summit of Carlton Peak. After a look at the upper falls, the Superior Hiking Trail veers to the right through the Superior National Forest. At around 2.5 miles, a short side trail provides a panoramic view of the lake and river valley. The trail circles to the right of the 100-foot-high rock wall summit. Lots of boulder debris to crawl over. The Superior Hiking Trail continues on to Britton Peak, while the Carlton Peak trail to the summit makes a sharp left. At the top you'll find the remains of a fire tower and a view of the lake from a staggering height of 1,526 feet. Even the eagles won't get in your way.

SCAVENGER HUNT (Cauldron Trail)

1. Basaltic (lava) rock

2. Hidden Falls

3. Cauldron gorge

4. Potholes

5. Upper Falls

TRIVIA QUESTIONS

Q: The Cauldron canyon is made up of many deep potholes all connected together. Thousands of years ago, churning glacial melt covered the entire North Shore and Great Lakes region. The water ran so wild and powerful it acted like giant drills boring sand and gravel into the soft lava, forming perfect potholes. Why are some of the potholes on the trail dry?

The dry potholes you see along the trail were once under a river, but the river changed course and became smaller.

Q: The Ojibwa Indians had a different name for the Temperance River. They called it "Kawimbash." What does that word mean?

"Kawimbash" means "deep hollow river."

Q: Carlton Peak is one of the North Shore's highest points. How high is it?

Carlton Peak is 1,526 feet high as compared with the Sears Tower in Chicago, which is 1,450 feet high.

Q: How many waterfalls are in Temperance River State Park?

There are three official waterfalls within the park.

Q: Part of the trail is over a large area of pockmarked gray rock. What kind of rock is this?

The rock found on the trail along the river is an ancient lava flow. The rock is called basaltic and it's more than a billion years old.

THINGS TO DO IN THE AREA

Naturalist Programs. Really cool, free 90-minute naturalist programs run all summer long, Tuesdays through Saturdays. Everyone is welcome, regardless of where you hang your hat for the night. They are sponsored by the USFS Superior National Forest, Lutsen-Tofte Tourism Association and the Grand Marais Area Tourism Association. Programs are held at various area lodges throughout the day. Join in on a campfire on the North Shore, take a wild-flower walk or visit a working lumber mill. There are 17 different programs. Contact one of the area chambers for more information (888-61NORTH), or log onto the Superior National Forest website for a program schedule at www.fs.fed.us/r9/forests/superior/recreation. (Click on "naturalist programs," then hit the "schedule" button for the North Shore programs.)

Sugarloaf Cove, Hwy 61 (4 miles south of Schroeder). Grab a trail map from the mailbox and hike the easy 1-mile trail through the woods, then head down to the beach for a picnic lunch. Along the shoreline, you'll find tons of round, flat stones that make perfect skippers.

Cross River State Wayside, Hwy 61, Schroeder. This waterfall is accessed right from the highway within the city limits. Trails lead down to the lake for a view of a cross erected in 1843 by Father Baraga, a missionary Catholic priest. Take a tour through the **Cross River Heritage Center** on Hwy 61 for the full story of the priest's life and harrowing journey across Lake Superior, as well as infor-mation about the area's rich fishing history. The Heritage Center is open June–October, closed Tues and Wed; 218-663-7706.

DINING

Coho Cafe, Bakery & Deli, Bluefin Bay, Hwy 61, Tofte; 218-663-8032; www.bluefinbay.com. Pizza, baked goods, soups, salads, sandwiches, desserts, espresso. Breakfast, lunch and dinner. **Cross River Cafe,** Hwy 61, Schroeder; 218-663-7208. Home-cooked meals and bakery.

LODGING

AmericInn Motel & Suites, 7231 W Hwy 61, Tofte; 800-625-7042 or 218-663-7899; www.americinntofte.com. Indoor pool and spa, free continental break-fast with Belgian waffles. **Bluefin Bay on Lake Superior,** PO Box 2125, Tofte; 800-BLUEFIN or 218-663-7296; www.bluefinbay.com. Indoor and outdoor pools and spas, tennis, on-site restaurants, bakery, gift shops. Hiking, biking and shuttle service. Open year-round. **Chateau Leveaux,** 6626 Hwy 61 W, Tofte; 800-445-5773 or 218-663-7223; www.chateauleveaux.com. Indoor pool and spa. Located on the shoreline of Lake Superior.

CAMPING

Temperance River State Park, 7620 West Hwy 61, Box 33, Schroeder; 218-663-7476. 55 campsites (18 electric), 3 cart-in. Hiking, fishing, waterfalls, ski and snowmobile trails. Lamb's Campground & Cabins, 4 Lambs Way & Hwy 61, Schroeder; 218-663-7292; www.lambsresort.com. 100 campsites with electricity, tent sites, log cabins on the lake, boat launch, private beach, bakery, restaurant and camp stores.

MORE STUFF

Lutsen-Tofte Visitor Information Center, 7136 W Hwy 61 (located inside the North Shore Commercial Fishing Museum at the Hwy 61 & Sawbill Trl intersection), Tofte; 888-61NORTH; www.61north.com. North Shore information plus trail maps for the 200-mile Superior Mountain Bike Trail System. The museum features fascinating local history about the founding Scandinavian fishermen and their way of life. Open year-round; small admission fee. Sawtooth Outfitters, 7213 Hwy 61, Tofte; 218-663-7643; www.sawtoothoutfitters.com. Equipment rental includes kayak, canoe, bike, snowshoes, cross-country skis/skates and downhill skis. Custom-guided trips available to BWCAW or Superior National Forest. Open year-round Tofte Charters, Tofte; 866-663-9932 or 218-663-9932; www.toftecharters.com. Lake Superior sport fishing and cruising. Superior Trails Sea Kayak Tours, Tofte; 218-663-0113. Equipment provided.

Hidden Falls

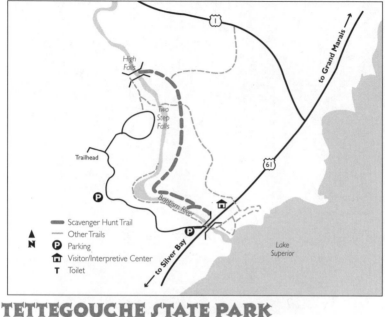

TETTEGOUCHE STATE PARK

POINTS OF INTEREST:
Waterfalls, suspension bridge, pristine scenery

TOTAL TRAIL MILES: 23
THIS HIKE: 2.75 miles (round-trip)
DIFFICULTY: Moderate
ELEVATION: 600 feet

After more than 80 years of private ownership, the nearly 8,500 acres of Tettegouche wilderness became an official state park in 1979. This park has something for everyone: six lakes, four waterfalls, the Baptism River, Lake Superior palisade shoreline, historic logging camp, the Sawtooth Mountains, ATV trails, mountain biking and a modern visitor center. The amazing scenery never ends, with one overlook more breathtaking than the next.

The park has 23 miles of rugged trails with a total elevation gain of 1,000 feet. There are four main paths: High Falls Trail, Shovel Point, a loop around Nicado, Nipisiquit, Mic Mac and Tettegouche Lakes and Mount Baldy and the Superior Hiking Trail, which cuts through the center of the park and takes in Mount Trudee and Bean and Bear Lakes. Some park highlights not to be missed: Shovel Point, the overlook of Mic Mac Lake and the incredible High Falls.

WHERE TO BEGIN

Tettegouche State Park is 4.5 miles northeast of Silver Bay on Hwy 61. The main park entrance is on the right. Pick up a trail map at the visitor center. The center has restrooms, drinking water and picnic areas. The picnic area also has an easy, self-guided interpretive trail with a couple cool Lake Superior overlooks. For those with toddlers, this may be about as much hiking as the kids will handle in this park. For the most part, the trails are loaded with steep climbs, tons of stairs and rocky terrain.

For a hike to the High Falls, drive south from the visitor center toward the campground and park in the small lot before the river (right side). You'll see the trailhead from there.

THE TRAILS

High Falls Of all the trails in the park, the 2.75-mile (round-trip) hike to the High Falls is probably the easiest. However, it will be a rather ambitious trek for those with young children. The trail is very well marked, but has lots of stairs and in places it's not much more than a cow path with encroaching plant life threatening to swallow it whole. In other places the trail is a twisting scramble over rocks and roots. There is a boardwalk through the wettest area. Butterflies and birds abound. This is a nature lover's paradise.

The Baptism River has two drops of 15 feet each, forming Two Steps Falls. There are about a gazillion steps leading down to the falls, but they are worth the huffing and puffing of the return climb. The 60-foot High Falls is another half mile farther on and joined by the Superior Hiking Trail. A suspension bridge crosses above the falls. where you can take a short loop back to the original trail or continue southwest on the Superior Hiking Trail.

SCAVENGER HUNT (High Falls Trail)

1. Coral fungi (not poisonous)

2. Birch burl

3 Two Steps Falls

4. High Falls

5. Suspension bridge

6. Rocks and roots on trail

7. Wild strawberry plants

TRIVIA QUESTIONS

Q: What is the name of the river that flows through Tettegouche State Park?

The Baptism River cuts through the park.

Q: "Tettegouche" is an old French-Canadian word. What does it mean?

"Tettegouche" means "meeting place."

Q: How high is the Baptism High Falls?

Baptism High Falls drops 60 feet, making it the second highest waterfall in Minnesota.

Q: How old are the rocks found in the park?

The gorge outcrops, Palisade Head, Shovel Point and the Sawtooth Mountains are really 1.1-billion-year-old basaltic lava flows.

Q: You can stay overnight in authentic log cabins found at Mic Mac Lake. Who built the cabins?

The log cabins found at Mic Mac Lake were built in 1898 by the Alger-Smith Lumber Company. After cutting down most of the Norway and white pines, the lumber company sold the camp in 1910 to the "Tettegouche Club," a group of businessmen from Duluth. Eventually, after two other owners, the land was established as a state park in 1979.

THINGS TO DO IN THE AREA

Beaver Bay, Hwy 61. Established in 1856, Beaver Bay is the oldest town along the North Shore. The beaches here are known as some of the best for stone skipping and agate hunting. Agates are small, multicolored, multilayered pebbles formed a billion years ago when minerals seeped into gas bubbles within the ancient lava flows. The kids will like the short hike on a boulder path to an island at East Beaver Bay. Take along some bread crumbs for the gulls.

Palisade Head, driving north on Hwy 61, watch for the sign located on the lake side immediately before Tettegouche State Park. This is the beginning point of more than 40 miles of the 350-foot-high North Shore palisades. Drive to the top for a sweeping view of the colorful cliffs guarding the Lake Superior shoreline. On a clear day you can see the Apostle Islands, which are more than 30 miles away. NOTE: Palisade Head offers only one lookout vantage with a stone wall to guard against falling. The rest of the area, though incredibly beautiful, can be dangerous for those with young children. Make sure you have a good grip on the little ones at all times.

Caribou Falls Wayside, Hwy 61 (heading north from Tettegouche State Park, the wayside is on the left). The 0.7 mile (one-way) trail to the falls stays fairly close to the Caribou River and is an incredibly scenic hike through the woods. It earns a moderate difficulty rating because most of the trail is a dirt footpath that winds up and over tree roots and gets pretty slippery along the river. But if you're looking for a short, interesting hike with a waterfall payoff, pull into the Caribou Falls Wayside. It is also a trailhead for the Superior Hiking Trail.

ATV Trails. There are almost 60 miles of ATV trails in the area of Silver Bay, Beaver Bay and Finland. They wind in and around lakes, around rock ledges and through hardwood forests and scenic overlooks of Lake Superior. ATV rentals are available at Beaver Bay Sport Shop (see information in the More Stuff section). The trails are open mid-May–Nov.

DINING

Wits' End Corner Country Store & Bakery, Hwy 61, Beaver Bay; 218-226-4074. Fresh baked breads and desserts, deli, made-to-order sandwiches, trail mixes, grocery supplies and a gift shop. Open year-round. Big Dipper, Beaver Bay Mini-Mall, Hwy 61, Beaver Bay; 218-226-3517. Sit back and enjoy some serious relaxing with a hand-dipped cone or one of the many other treats served at the Big Dipper. Open mid-May–mid-Oct.

LODGING

AmericInn Lodge & Suites, 150 Mensing Dr, Silver Bay; 800-634-3444 or 218-226-4300; www.americinn.com. Indoor pool, 110-foot waterslide, wading pool and spa. Recreation room and free continental breakfast. Cove Point Lodge, 4614 Hwy 61, Beaver Bay; 800-598-3221 or 218-226-3221; www.covepoint-lodge.com. Pool and spa, free use of canoes and snowshoes. Lodge and cottages available. Open year-round. Illgen Falls Cabin, located within the eastern edge of Tettegouche State Park; 218-226-6365. The drive-to, 2 bedroom cabin has a fireplace, complete kitchen and gas grill. The large deck overlooks the 45-foot-high Illgen Falls. The cabin sleeps 6 and is handicapped accessible.

CAMPING

Tettegouche State Park, 5702 Hwy 61 E, Silver Bay; 218-226-6365. 34 drive-in campsites (no electricity), 13 cart-in sites, 6 backpack sites, 1 kayak site. Also 4 authentic log cabins on Mic Mac Lake accessed by a 1.7-mile hike/bike trail. Cabins have 2-burner electric cook tops and small refrigerators and come with a canoe. No running water, but there is a hand pump and shower building. Open year-round. **George H. Crosby Manitou State Park**, 474 Hwy 61 E (from Hwy 61 at Illgen City, drive north on Hwy 1 for 7 miles to Cty 7, drive northeast 7 miles), Silver Bay; 218-226-3539 or 218-226-6365 (managed by Tettegouche State Park). 21 primitive walk-in campsites, no drinking water, 24 miles of rugged scenic trails, 8 waterfalls and trout fishing. **Eckbeck Campground**, from Hwy 61 in Illgen City, drive north on Hwy 1 for 3 miles; 218-226-6365. 30 primitive drive-in sites, outhouses, drinking water, hiking and fishing. **Finland Campground**, from Hwy 61 in Illgen City, drive north on Hwy 1 for 6 miles, then east on Cty 6 for less than ½ mile; 218-226-6365. 39 primitive drive-in sites, boat launch, outhouses, drinking water, hiking and fishing.

MORE STUFF

Beaver Bay/Silver Bay Area Chamber of Commerce, 610 East-West Rd, Silver Bay; 218-226-4870. **Grampa Woo/Lake Superior Excursions**, Hwy 61, Beaver Bay; 218-226-4100 or 251-421-4211; www.grampawoo.com. **Fugitive Charters**, 86 Hays Circle, Silver Bay; 218-226-3638. Lake Superior sport fishing. **Beaver Bay Sports Shop**, Hwy 61, Beaver Bay; 218-226-4666; www.BeaverBaySports.com. Bike, ATV and snowmobile rentals.

Suspension bridge

TETTEGOUCHE STATE PARK **135**

WHAT YOU SHOULD KNOW

Let's face it: kids, sooner or later, get hurt. Luckily, most injuries are not serious and can be handled with a basic first aid kit. Sometimes, though, you might need to handle an emergency. This section covers all the stuff my friends and I wish we'd known when we first started taking our kids on hikes. It's impossible to prepare for absolutely everything that you could encounter when you go hiking, but I've included the most common.

WHAT TO DO IN A REAL EMERGENCY

- STAY CALM. Your child will take his/her cue from you.
- Call 911.
- Start CPR if your child is not breathing.
- If bleeding, apply continuous pressure to the site with a clean cloth.
- If your child is having a seizure, lay the child down on the floor or ground with his/her head turned to the side. DO NOT put anything in his/her mouth.
- Do not move your injured child unless he/she is in immediate danger.
- Stay with your child until help arrives.

FIRST AID TRAINING AND RESOURCES

SciVolutions's easy-to-use online first aid guide covers just about every situation and incident that may occur, plus it also includes detailed CPR instructions complete with diagrams. www.firstaidguide.net

The Harvard Medical School Family Health Guide provides practical suggestions for stocking your first aid kit, as well as procedures to follow for the top ten emergencies. www.health.harvard.edu

The American Red Cross' online store features fully stocked first aid kits and reference handbooks that cover everything from medical emergencies to pet first aid. First aid and CPR classes are offered through the American Red Cross. Check their website for class locations nearest you. www.redcross.org

The Safety Store has a nice selection of wilderness emergency care books. Order online or call for a catalog. www.safetystore.com or 888-723-3897

HEAD INJURIES

Bumps, scrapes and bruises can be constant companions when your child is active. Most injuries are not life-threatening. But when it comes to head injuries, you should call your health care provider for anything more than a light bump.

How do you know whether a head injury requires medical attention? If your child is alert and responds to you, the injury is most likely mild. Apply a cold compress to the area and observe your child for a period of time to make sure nothing serious develops.

Signs of a more serious head injury:

According to information found on Medline Plus (the U.S. National Library of Medicine and the National Institutes of Health website www.nlm.nih.gov/medlineplus), the following are symptoms of what could be a serious head injury:

• A constant headache that gets worse
• Cannot stop crying
• Slurred speech
• Dizziness that does not go away or reoccurs
• Vomiting more than twice
• Clumsiness or difficulty walking
• Oozing blood or watery fluid from the nose or ears
• Becomes drowsy and has difficulty waking
• Unequal pupil size
• Unusual paleness that lasts for more than 1 hour
• Confusion or unusual behavior
• Seizures or convulsions

If your child displays any of these symptoms, seek immediate medical attention. This information does not apply to children younger than 2 years of age. If your child is under 2 years old, seek medical attention for all head injuries.

DEHYDRATION

According to the Mayo Clinic, 60 percent of your body weight is made up of water. Each day your body recycles water during its normal physiological functions. It loses 6–10 glasses of water during this process. Normal loss of body fluid includes sweating, urinating and breathing. Dehydration occurs when the body loses too much water.

The Mayo Clinic website says kids do not handle heat and humidity as well as adults. They produce more heat, sweat less and may be less likely to drink enough fluids during exercise—all of which increase their risk of dehydration.

Preventing dehydration:

Thirst is the way the body indicates it is already dehydrated. Drink to prevent thirst, not to quench it! During hot and humid weather, the American Academy of Pediatrics (AAP) recommends making children drink 5 ounces of water every 15–20 minutes (9 ounces for adolescents) even if they aren't feeling thirsty. Reduce intense physical activity lasting more than 15 minutes. Take rest periods in the shade to cool off and watch for signs of dehydration. For infants and young children, take Pedialyte (or a good electrolyte replacement fluid) on the hike and encourage them to sip it. For more information about the prevention and warning signs of dehydration, check out the Mayo Clinic website (www.MayoClinic.com).

SUNBURNS

According to the American Academy of Pediatrics, the best line of defense against sunburn is covering up. (Tanning oils and baby oils do not protect against sunburn.) They recommend a hat with a three-inch brim, sunglasses that block 100 percent of UV rays, and light-colored, tightly-woven cotton clothing. Stay in the shade when possible and avoid exposure during peak hours when the sun is the most intense (10am–4pm). Be aware that risk of sunburn increases in higher altitudes. If your child does get sunburned, cool the area with cold running water or apply a cold compress. Do not use ice on a sunburn as it may delay healing, and do not rub the area as it can increase blistering.

Are sunscreens safe for children?

The American Academy of Pediatrics does not recommend using a sunscreen on infants under 6 months old. They do recommend dressing infants in light-weight long pants, long-sleeved shirts and brimmed hats, and stress keeping them out of the sun. If adequate shade is not an option, a very minimal amount of sunscreen may be applied to exposed skin, but never on the hands, as infants tend to put them in their mouths.

For young children, use a sunscreen with an SPF of 15 or greater. Reapply every 2 hours and after swimming. Sunscreens should be applied before insect repellent is applied. For more information about the application of sunscreens, log onto the American Academy of Pediatrics' website (www.aap.org).

MOSQUITOES AND TICKS

There are mosquitoes, ticks, black flies, fleas and no-see-'ems in the woods. They are attracted to our body heat, the chemicals in our sweat and the carbon dioxide expelled by our breathing. Other insect attractors are particular clothing textures and colors, soap scents, perfumes, lotions and hair care products.

What you can do to avoid mosquito bites:

Mosquitoes are drawn to strong scents and dark colors. Wear light-colored, tightly-woven, long-sleeved shirts and pants and use unscented hygiene products. Their prime feeding time is dusk to dawn, so plan hikes accordingly. Protect infants with mosquito netting.

Ticks:

It's a fact—you will encounter ticks in the wilderness. It is their home. Ticks can carry disease; therefore, it is always wise to have a doctor look at a tick bite, should one occur. A red, circular bump or rash and/or flu symptoms may indicate (but not always) you were bitten by a tick carrying Lyme Disease. To remove a tick from your skin, use a pair of tweezers and get as close to the tick's head as possible, then gently pull the tick out. Wash the bite area with soap and water. For more information about ticks, go to www.nlm.nih.gov/medlineplus/tickbites.

Are insect repellents safe for children?

According to the United States Department of Public Health, DEET is one of the most common and effective ingredients in insect repellents. However, it may be toxic, especially to young children. They recommend using products with 10 percent (or less) DEET. Do not use repellents on children younger than 2 years. Do not use products containing oil of lemon or eucalyptus on children 3 years and younger. Never use products that contain permethrin or malathion. These are extremely toxic when exposed to the skin.

Never apply repellents on a child's hands; kids tend to stick them in their mouths and eyes. Never apply repellent directly on a child and never spray the product on his/her face. Apply the repellent to your own hands and then rub them on your child. Use a single light coating of repellent. Avoid overexposure by washing off all repellent with soap and water before reapplying. Spray clothing before your child puts it on so they do not inhale the repellent, and never apply the product in an enclosed area. Always wash off repellent when finished with outdoor activity.

If a child has an adverse reaction to a repellent, immediately wash his/her skin with soap and water and call your health care provider or the Poison Control Center (800-222-1222). If you go to a doctor or hospital, take the repellent with you.

For more information about insect repellents, call the National Pesticide Information Center (800-858-7378). Other good sources of information include the Environmental Protection Agency's website (www.epa.gov/pesticides/health/mosquitoes) and the Centers for Disease Control and Prevention (www.cdc.gov/ncidod/dvbid/westnile/index.htm).

BEE STINGS

Bright colors and flowery prints attract bees and other insects, so when possible, avoid these clothing choices. (Be aware that DEET products will not repel stinging insects.) To remove a visible stinger, gently scrape it off horizontally with a credit card or your fingernail. Put ice or a cold compress on the affected area to decrease pain and swelling. If your child shows signs of an allergic reaction, including labored breathing, faintness and hives, get immediate medical attention. Check out the Mayo Clinic's website for other signs of allergic reaction (www.MayoClinic.com).

POISON IVY

It's a law of the universe that if poison ivy is anywhere within a ten-mile radius of your kids, they will find it—so be prepared.

What does poison ivy look like?

Poison ivy proliferates in three forms: vine, bush and ground cover. It has three leaves per cluster. This plant has an almost attractive appearance, especially in the fall when its leaves turn red. A simple guide to identifying these noxious plants is: leaves of three, let it be. Make this your family's mantra before every hike.

Yikes, I touched poison ivy!

Poison ivy leaves contain a very potent oil called urushiol. It takes a surprisingly tiny amount of oil to cause a rash. You have 15 minutes to remove the oil before it bonds to the skin. The best way to deactivate the oil is to rinse the skin with cold water for at least 5 minutes. If water is not available, rubbing alcohol is also effective. DO NOT use a washcloth as it will spread the oil.

Help! I have a poison ivy rash!

For first-time poison ivy sufferers, it may take up to 10 days before red itchy welts and blisters appear. Most people break out within 24–48 hours (4–12 hours for sensitive persons). Rubbing the rash will not spread it to other parts of the body. Poison ivy is not contagious. Hot showers, as hot as tolerable, will bring temporary relief of the itch. Corticosteroids reduce the swelling. See your doctor for treatment.

The Poison Ivy, Oak & Sumac Information Center is an invaluable Internet resource. Log onto their website (www.poisonivy.us) for great pictures of plants, remedies, helpful links and a viewer collection of rashes—definitely not for the squeamish.

OTHER NOXIOUS PLANTS

An encounter with poison ivy or other rash-causing plants may be painful, but Minnesota is also home to some plants that can be downright harmful. Check out the USDA Plants Database for pictures and identification information (http://plants.usda.gov/index.html).

Poison oak, like poison ivy, has three leaves and can cause a rash.

Poison sumac grows in swamps and bogs. The compound leaves are made up of 7–13 leaflets. Its oils are toxic and cause a rash.

Wild parsnip is another common Minnesota plant found in ditches along roadsides and other wet areas. Wild parsnip is not fatal, but causes a nasty, blister rash when touched—especially when skin is exposed to sunlight.

Poison hemlock is one of the most dangerous plants in the United States. It has a yellow, oily discharge, and ALL parts are poisonous: leaves, stem, roots and especially the seeds. Poison from this plant causes severe depression of the nervous system, paralysis and death.

Water hemlock's root smells like a carrot, but ingesting even a small amount of this plant will cause nervousness, breathing difficulties, muscle tremors, convulsions and death.

MUSHROOMS

Mushrooms are the fleshy growths of fungus, which are thread-like fibers grow-ing in soil, wood or decaying materials. Their purpose is to produce spores or "fungus seeds." Since many types of mushrooms grow in the woods, chances are your kids will find some.

Not all wild mushrooms are poisonous. In fact, many are edible. But unless you are a mushroom and fungus expert, the best thing to do is tell your kids to leave ALL mushrooms alone. For more information about mushrooms, log onto: http://mdc.mo.gov/nathis/mushrooms/

HERBICIDES

Kids have a natural curiosity about everything. Nothing escapes their scrutiny or their little hands. A word of caution: avoid contact with plants along hiking/biking trails and main roads as they may be sprayed with herbicides.

SNAKES

There are seventeen snake species in Minnesota and only two are poisonous: the timber rattlesnake and the massasauga or swamp rattler. Chances of seeing either of these species are rare. The best ways to avoid being bitten by any snake are to leave all snakes alone and keep your hands and feet out of places you cannot see into, such as holes or hollow logs. There are several very reliable ways to differentiate between poisonous and nonpoisonous snakes. Nonpoisonous snakes have a tail that comes to a point like a sharpened pencil, a round pupil and no pit between the eye and nostril. Poisonous snakes have a cat-eye (elliptical) pupil and large heat pits between their eyes and nostrils that serve as sensors to help them detect their prey's body heat. Links to pictures and descriptions of all of Minnesota's reptiles (and amphibians too) can be found on the Minnesota Herpetological Society's website (www.bellmuseum.org/her-petology/main.html).

First aid for a snake bite:

If bitten, call the Poison Control Center immediately (800-222-1222). They will help determine if the snake was poisonous and provide expert first aid advice. The Mayo Clinic also has first aid advice for snake bite (www.MayoClinic.com).

If you will be unable to get medical attention within 30 minutes, the American Red Cross recommends applying a bandage 2–4 inches above the bite to help slow the effects of the venom. The bandage should be loose enough to slide a finger beneath it.

RESOURCES

Minnesota Poison Control System: 800-222-1222 (emergency line) or www.mnpoison.org. Great information about everything from sunscreen protection to bicycle safety, as well as what to do if your child comes in contact with, or ingests, a poisonous substance.

Minnesota Department of Natural Resources: 888-MINNDNR (888-646-6367) or (651) 296-6157 or www.dnr.state.mn.us. Information on state parks, trails, fishing, lakes and rivers.

DNR Trails & Waterways: (651) 297-1151 or www.dnr.state.mn.us. Lake Superior water trail maps and other helpful canoe and boating guides.

Minnesota Office of Tourism: 888-TOURISM (888-868-7476) or (651) 296-5029 or www.exploreminnesota.com. Information on places to stay and things to do.

Minnesota Historical Society: 888-727-8386 or www.mnhs.org. Information on state historical sites and events.

Minnesota Department of Transportation: 800-542-0220 or 511-542-0220 or www.511mn.org. Information regarding road construction and weather-related road conditions.

Travel Deals: Many Minnesota cities offer special package deals that add up to big savings on hotels, restaurants, attractions, theatre tickets, shuttle services and more. Contact the local chamber of commerce of the city nearest the area you wish to visit and ask about their package deals.

HELPFUL WEBSITES

www.MNBIKETRAILS.com This is a great resource for biking news, including information on paved trails.

www.trails.com This site lists the top 20 hiking trails in the state. Some of the trails are challenging, multi-day hikes and not suited for young children. For adults with rugged stamina and the curiosity of Louis Sinclair, these trails will provide a welcome challenge.

www.minnesotahotelsonline.com A listing of Minnesota hotels/motels.

www.minnesotacampgroundsonline.com Skip the phone call and reserve a spot at your favorite campground online.

www.minnesotaresortsonline.com Plan your vacation online at a favorite resort.

www.hospitalitymn.com This website provides a listing of hotels/motels, lodges and campgrounds.

www.northshorevisitor.com Online vacation and lodging guide for the North Shore region of Lake Superior.

www.northshoreinfo.com/lodging/camping.htm Detailed information on all lodging and campgrounds, private and public, including state parks, state forests and the Superior National Forest/BWCAW. State and national forests sites are reserved on a first-come-first-served policy.

www.tourminnesota.org Online information guide featuring attractions, dining, lodging, tours and transportation.

www.arborday.org Cool site with a section called Kids Explore Club that features family outdoor activities.

STATE PARK INFORMATION

RULES, VEHICLE FEES AND CAMPSITE RESERVATIONS

Annual vehicle permit fees for Minnesota State Parks are nominal and a good value. Daily permits are even cheaper. Many parks offer rustic (tent) sites, modern to semi-modern campsites and sites accommodating horses for a small additional fee.

Gathering firewood is not permitted—it disrupts the forest and the soil cycle. You can usually purchase firewood at the park office.

Pets are allowed in all Minnesota State Parks, but must be on a leash no longer than six feet and attended at all times. Pets are not allowed in buildings, on tours or in beach areas. You must clean up after your pet. Seeing-eye dogs and other service animals are permitted in all areas.

Privately owned land exists within many park and trail boundaries. Check with the park manager first before using facilities, trails and roads not on official park/trail maps.

Finally, respect nature. Do not dig, pick, pluck or take any rock, plant, bug, seed or animal from its habitat. In this way, everyone can enjoy our state's natural wonders for generations to come. For camping reservations: call 866-85PARKS (866-857-2757) (TDD 866-290-2267) or reserve online at www.stayatmnparks.com

STATE PARK SCAVENGER HUNTS

You can purchase a Hiking Club Kit or a Passport Club Kit at any of the state parks for a reasonable price. This purchase enrolls your child in a fun scavenger hunt. There is a secret word hidden in plain sight on every state park Blue Diamond Hiking Club trail. Find the secret word and get a stamp. Collect eight stamps and earn a free overnight stay in any state park.

A full-blooded Irish lass, Mary M. Bauer was born and raised in Lutefisk Country. She and her husband jumped the state line over a dozen years ago and bought a Wisconsin dairy farm. Her two children ran off to college, then found careers to avoid baling hay and fence painting. A former nurse and interior designer, Mary began her writing career as a weekly columnist for a regional newspaper. She discovered ranting in public and getting paid for it is a lot of fun. She is the author of Adventure Publication's *Minnesota Day Trips by Theme* and *Wisconsin's Day Trips by Theme*. Besides family, her major loves are traveling, hiking, books, decrepit Christmas decorations and Reese's Peanut Butter Cups. She is a dog and cat person, and is thinking about adopting a pig.